abortion:
the
SILENT
HOLOCAUST

John Powell, S.J.

Argus Communications
Allen, Texas 75002 U.S.A.

ACKNOWLEDGMENTS

Excerpts from "Medical Practice Under Dictatorship" by Leo Alexander, in *The New England Journal of Medicine*, July 14, 1949, pp 39–46. Reprinted by permission of *The New England Journal of Medicine*.

Excerpt from a letter to "Fellow Christians" from Dr. Harold O. J. Brown, chairman of the Christian Action Council, December 1, 1975. Reprinted by permission of Dr. Brown.

Continued on page 183

Photo Credits

Michael Abramson/BLACK STAR 45
J. Baker/ALPHA 168
David Barnes/PHOTO RESEARCHERS 116
Lawrence Cherney/SHOSTAL ASSOCIATES 36
Randy Dieter 97
Nelson Kniffin//SHOSTAL ASSOCIATES 105
R. Llewellyn/BRUCE COLEMAN 85, 156
Jan Lukas/PHOTO RESEARCHERS 65
Jay Lurie/BRUCE COLEMAN 73
Fred Maroon/PHOTO RESEARCHERS 144
Sue Ann Miller/BLACK STAR 132
Dick Patterson/SHOSTAL ASSOCIATES 172
Bruce Roberts/PHOTO RESEARCHERS 4, 25
Marilyn Sanders/PETER ARNOLD 80
THREE LIONS 17
Richard Watherwax/FPG 124
Willinger/FPG 9
Jonathan T. Wright/BRUCE COLEMAN 53

Cover by Gene Tarpey Design

Argus Communications
A Division of DLM, Inc.
One DLM Park
Allen, Texas 75002 U.S.A.

International Standard Book Number: 0-89505-063-3
Library of Congress Number: 81-69697

0 9 8 7 6 5 4 3 2 1

DEDICATION

The pages of this book are dedicated to every woman who is carrying a child under her heart . . . especially if your heart is trembling with fear or is crushed beneath a lonely grief.

Please believe that you are not alone. There are many of us who truly love you, who want to stand at your side, and help in any way we can.

CONTENTS

"Although every holocaust ever perpetrated is an unprecedented event in its own right, this should not detract from what all holocausts share in common . . . the systematic and widespread destruction of millions looked upon as indiscriminate masses of subhuman expendables.

"The cultural environment for a human holocaust is present whenever any society can be misled into defining individuals as less than human and therefore devoid of value and respect."

—William Brennan,
from *Medical Holocaust*
(Nordland Publishing, 1980)

A Grim Memorial Day Reminder of American War Casualties

Each cross-mark represents 50,000 people killed. The war casualties represent all American combat and combat-related deaths.

Revolutionary War (25,324) . . . . †

Civil War (498,332) . . . . †††††††††

World War I (116,516) . . . . ††┤

World War II (545,108) . . . . ††††††††††

Korean War (54,246) . . . . †

Vietnam War (56,555) . . . . †

WAR OF ANOTHER KIND—WAR ON THE UNBORN. 12,000,000 killed by legalized abortion, as of January 1981. In excess of 1,500,000 more expected annually.
The U.S. Supreme Court legalized abortion on 22 January 1973.

††††††††††
††††††††††
††††††††††
††††††††††
††††††††††

†††††††††††††††††† ††††††††††
†††††††††††††††††††† ††††††††††
†††††††††††††††††††††† ††††††††
††††††††††††††††††††††††††††
††††††††††††††††††††††††††††
†††††††††††††††††††††††††††††
†††††††††††††††††††††††††††††
††††††††††

Statistics compiled by Barbara Syska, Research Analyst, National Right to Life Committee.

OF LIFE AND LOVE
AND LONELINESS
A Chapter of My Life,
A Burden on My Heart

The greatest gift of God,
I would think,
is the gift of life.

The greatest sin of humans,
it would seem,
would be to return that gift
ungratefully and unopened.

No man is an island. . . . Any man's death diminishes
me, because I am involved in mankind; and therefore never send to know for whom the bell tolls; it
tolls for thee.

—John Donne

1

My Dear Sisters and Brothers
in the Human Family:

Whenever I have written in the past, my inspiration has always been the sheer excitement of a new insight and a desire to share that insight with you. I come to you now more lonely and frightened than excited. I ask you to share with me the sadness and fear that I am experiencing. As the Irish orator Edmund Burke once said, "An event is happening about which it is difficult to speak but about which it is impossible to remain silent." This is a book I cannot not write. Silence would be unbearable.

Somehow I feel sure that most of you, good and decent as you are, don't want to read or hear any more about abortion, infanticide, and euthanasia. In this area convictions are in conflict, emotions are raw, and the words of discussion have become shrill.

So I would ask you, as a favor to me and ultimately as a favor to yourself, to stay with me. I would ask you to let me share with you something about myself and where I am. It may be that you are not where I am. It is all right for us to be in different places. Each of us must march to a personal drummer. In the end it may be that you will not be able to share my beliefs, nor I yours, but it will be good for both of us to have listened to each other. In such dialogue, there is no win-lose contest. In such sharing everyone is a winner because everyone is enriched.

Mahatma Ghandi once said that the main duty of everyone in the course of his/her life is to keep sifting through and searching for permanent values. Eventually, he said, we must fix on the value that really matters. I have a sense that my whole life, whether I knew it or not, has been involved with this work of sifting priorities. Following the rhythms of my own drummer, in the place that I now find myself, I am certain that each and every human life has an absolute value. With all my mind and heart and strength I am *pro-life:* Wherever there is a flower of life I want it to bloom, to reveal its beauty for all the world to see. I believe that each and every one of us is a unique and unrepeatable creation. There are no carbon copies. We are all "originals" from the mind and heart of God.

Each of Us Is a Message

There is an old Judeo-Christian tradition that God sends each person into this world with a special message to deliver, with a special song to sing, with a special act of love to bestow. No one else can speak my message, or sing my song, or bestow my act of love. These have been entrusted only to me.

According to this tradition, the message may be spoken, the song sung, the act of love delivered only to a few, or to all the folk in a small village, or to all the people in a large city, or even to all the people in the whole world. Everything depends on God's unique plan for each unique person.

As I see it, to be pro-life means to be open to the unique gift that every human being is, to be open to hear the song and to take into gentle hands the gift of that person's love.

To take an innocent life deliberately is to say a violent "NO!" to a unique and unrepeatable human being. "I will not hear your message . . .

I will not listen to your song . . . I do not want your love . . . I will not give you my love." To take a life is a rejection of a human person; it is a rejection of the message, the song, and the love entrusted to that person by God.

The Loneliness of the Pro-life Runner

> We hold these truths to be self-evident, that all men are created equal, that they are endowed by their Creator with certain unalienable Rights, that among these are Life, Liberty and the pursuit of Happiness.
> —The Declaration of Independence, July 4, 1776

Each day in our country over four thousand human lives are ended by abortion. The numbers continue to multiply, and already in cities like New York and Washington, D.C., there are more life-ending abortions than live births. It is expected that this will soon become a national pattern and be true in all our large cities. This massive rejection of life is the greatest sadness and the deepest loneliness that have ever entered my life. Carl Jung once said of loneliness that it does not result from the absence of people around us, but is experienced when the people around us do not understand what is going on inside us. In this age of abortion-on-demand, I have come to know the meaning of loneliness.

When people ask me why it bothers me so much that there are more than four thousand abortions each day in this country, I am reminded of a story from the life of Martin Luther King. Once he was jailed for protesting the denial of equality to black Americans. Someone asked him: "Why are you in jail?" His only response was: "Why are you *not* in

5

jail?'' The sadness and loneliness inside me make me want to ask those who question me: "Why are you *not* bothered?"

The year was 1776. In the broiling chambers of the Continental Congress in Philadelphia, the American dream of independence was tipped on end. It could have fallen either way: into the brave new future of a free nation or back into the subhuman subservience of a colony and colonialism. In the stage play *1776*, John Adams is portrayed at this critical moment of history as a lonely figure, pacing in frustration during the dark night. He knows that the American dream could die in the hot belly and in the deadlocked debates of the congressional chambers. Hope was hanging by a thread and he knew it. The heart of John Adams is filled with anguish. His guts ache with three lonely questions:

> Is anyone there?
> Does anyone see what I see?
> Does anyone care?

As I live through this dark night of a failing reverence for the sanctity of life, my own guts are moaning these same three questions: Is anyone there? Does anyone see what I see? Does anyone care?

Love: The Only Way to Go

As I sift through my own priorities and values, I consider that the fundamental option of my life is that I have chosen to make *love* the motive of my life. I want my life and all that I do somehow to be an act of love. Of course, I am fragile and I fail, but this is my ideal, my life wager. At all the cross-roads of life and in all the moments of decision, I want only to ask: "What is the loving thing to do, to be, to say?" So I want my pro-life stance to be an act of love. Anger, hatred, and vengeance are sirens of seduction which can only mislead us.

Anger eats away at the angry; hatred destroys the hater. Vengeance is a psychological cancer. Negative motivation and emotions wear out. They end in bitterness. As a motive and emotion, love is susceptible of continual growth. It blossoms into beauty not bitterness.

When we react bitterly to the bitter, deceitfully to the deceiving, we have allowed them to decide how we are going to act. We have to an extent put our lives in their hands. We have put our decisions and our happiness in their control. We have been reactors rather than actors. For me it seems very necessary that those who join in the pro-life effort should strive to be actors not reactors, lovers not haters, and in all things truthful. Of course, it is not always an easy way to go, but it is the only way to go. The whole pro-life effort is either an act of love or it is nothing.

I remember once watching a local television talk show. The discussion was abortion, and the opposing sides were carefully positioned on opposite sides of the table. On the pro-life side were two men for whom I have an enormous admiration. They are U.S. Congressman Henry J. Hyde from Illinois and Dr. Victor G. Rosenblum, a professor of law and political science at Northwestern University. Dr. Rosenblum is a lawyer who is also affiliated with the American Civil Liberties Union, which is curiously pro-abortion-on-demand. (I say

7

"curiously" because I've always thought that any group seriously interested in defending the civil liberties of the defenseless would certainly want to champion the rights of the unborn.)

In the course of the discussion, Hyde and Rosenblum repeatedly underlined the fact that the unborn child represents a human life. The child is "one of us." Then someone from the other side of the table asked Dr. Rosenblum if he would permit an abortion if it were medically established that the baby was defective or would be retarded. Obviously, the questioner did not know that Dr. Rosenblum has a retarded child, whom he loves very much. At any rate his response was, "Oh no, no, no." And then Dr. Rosenblum continued:

> Do you believe in love? I don't mean simple lip service to love. I am talking about life service. Do you really believe that we are here to love one another? If you do, then you don't say, "I will love *you* because you have your mental faculties, and *you* because you are healthy, but *not you* because you have only one arm." True love does not discriminate in this way.

> If we really believe in love, and find that a baby will be born having no arms, we would say, "Baby, we are going to love you. We will make arms for you. We have many new skills now for doing this. And, Baby, if these arms don't work, we will *be* your arms. We will take care of you. You can be sure of that. You are one of us, a member of our human family, and we will always love you." [paraphrased]

The questioner didn't know what to do with that response. What do you do with someone who really knows what it means to love? So he asked Dr. Rosenblum if he thought the furor would die down if enough people have abortions and talk

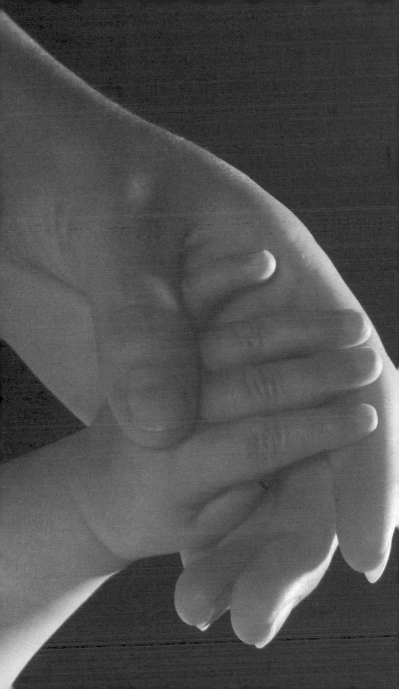

openly about them. I remember well how the great, good, and decent man that is Victor Rosenblum lowered his head and whispered, "Yes. Yes, it will, and that will be the saddest day in American history."

I think Dr. Rosenblum is a man who is motivated by and knows the meaning of love. In my own pro-life efforts, I want to be like him—an actor not a reactor, *for something* rather than *against someone*. I have always believed that one person who truly loves is somehow a majority and somehow invincible.

The Day of the Decision

On January 22, 1973—a day which will always be "Black Monday" for me—I was driving a car along a Chicago expressway, listening to the news. The voice of the announcer said it fluently and easily, but it hit me with all the suddenness of a heart attack: "The Supreme Court of the United States has legalized abortion-on-demand." The newscaster continued to spell out the details, but the computer of my mind got jammed by the initial announcement. I couldn't absorb the details. It was like going into shock. Something in me refused to believe what my ears had heard. I bought a late edition of the newspapers to verify the shocking, unbelievable decision. It was, of course, true. A new ethic was legally instituted by the Supreme Court of the United States. A new era of my own life was begun.

In two separate decisions (*Roe* v. *Wade* and *Doe* v. *Bolton*), the Supreme Court ruled that any state abortion law in the future would have to meet certain guidelines. The following is my own summary of the Court ruling:

First trimester: During the first three months of pregnancy, the state must leave the abortion decision entirely to a woman and her physician.

Second trimester: During the second three months, the state may only enact laws which regulate abortions in ways "reasonably related to maternal health." This simply means that a state may determine who is qualified to perform the abortion and where the abortion may take place. The state may not, however, enact any laws which safeguard the lives of the unborn.

Third trimester: After the woman's sixth or seventh month of pregnancy, the law may forbid her to have an abortion that is not determined to be necessary to preserve her "life or health." The Court went on to define the word *health* in such broad terms—i.e., social well-being—as to make it virtually impossible for a state to protect the unborn child even after the sixth or seventh month of pregnancy.

Actually the Court did not use the terms *first, second,* and *third trimester* as given above. It rather speaks of *viability* as the operative term after the first trimester. In the words of the Court:

(a) For the stage prior to approximately the end of the first trimester, the abortion decision and its effectuation must be left to the medical judgment of the pregnant woman's attending physician.

(b) For the stage subsequent to approximately the end of the first trimester, the State, in promoting its interest in the health of the mother, may, if it chooses, regulate the abortion procedure in ways that are reasonably related to maternal health.

(c) For the stage subsequent to viability, the State, in promoting its interest in the potentiality of human life, may, if it chooses, regulate, and even proscribe, abortion except where it is necessary, in appropriate medical judgment, for the preservation of the life or health of the mother. [from *Roe* v. *Wade*, Syllabus p. 49, Justice Blackmun delivering the opinion of the Court, January 22, 1973]

And so the justices of the Supreme Court, in open disregard of prior legal tradition and contrary to overwhelming biological evidence and to the ethical traditions of a majority of the American people, struck down the abortion laws of all fifty states (even the most permissive at the time). The justices of the Court made abortion-on-demand, at every stage of pregnancy, the law of the land. On January 22, 1973, the Court gave the United States the dubious distinction of having the most permissive abortion laws of any nation in the Western world.

In subsequent ruling, the Court carried this massive but legal assault on life to the institution of marriage and to the structure of the family. In *Planned Parenthood of Central Missouri* v. *Danforth*, the Court ruled that a wife may obtain an abortion without her husband's consent. In the same opinion the Court held unconstitutional Missouri's law requiring parental consent prior to a minor's abortion. In most states a minor is still required to have parental consent before leaving home, marrying, getting a job, undergoing surgery, attending adult movies, or even getting her ears pierced. However, the Supreme Court made it clear that she can have an abortion without any such parental permission. In this decision the Court seemed to disregard the parents' natural interest in and responsibility for their daughter's physical and emotional health, their daughter's conduct and formation of conscience, and, of course, their grandchild.

The moral sadness of all this is that most people regard the law as a teacher. For most Americans what is legal is also moral. It was Supreme Court Justice Louis Brandeis who observed in 1928 that "our government is the potent, the omnipresent teacher. For good or for ill, it teaches the whole people by its example."

Of course I have my own personal wrinkles, but I have always thought of myself as somehow strangely immune from two afflictions so often presented in counseling situations: loneliness and depression. I always listened carefully to descriptions of these, trying to experience by empathy and vicariously these burdens from which I had seemingly been spared. Since January 22, 1973— and I don't say this for dramatic effect—I have felt the touch of depression and loneliness described by Jung. I hear John Adams's questions from a place deep down inside myself: "Is anyone there? Does anyone see what I see? Does anyone care?"

The Call to Action

I have searched my heart and my life experience for an explanation of this very painful response to the abortion legislation and its results. My first recourse was to pray for enlightenment. Face to face with God in prayer, I felt a clear call out of apathy and into action. As I listened to my own emotional response to such a vocation, I heard in myself something of the reluctance of young Jeremiah when God called him to become a prophet. He was young and green. He probably stuttered, and he had little inclination for the inevitable conflict. But wanting it or not, God wanted him. I had the same sense of being wanted.

At the same time I felt something in me of the prophet Isaiah. God asked, "Whom shall I send?" Isaiah quickly responded, "Here I am. Send me." Both prophetic reactions, reluctance and readiness, rose out of the depths of my own mind and heart.

I also thoughtfully reviewed my life experiences and found two, among others, which have left me with an acute sensitivity to the value of every human life. I would like to share something of these two experiences with you, even though I am aware that such profound experiences are essentially incommunicable. Nevertheless these two experiences remain very much a part of me and of my story.

CHAPTER 2

FROM AKRON TO DACHAU
From Human Ecstasy
to Human Agony

"To me, the nations with legalized abortions are the poorest nations. The great destroyer of peace today is the crime against the innocent unborn child. . . .

"In destroying the child, we are destroying love, destroying the image of God in the world."

—Mother Teresa of Calcutta,
  awarded the Nobel Peace Prize,
  1979

The Birth of a Baby Boy

It was at the end of my fifteen years of Jesuit training. I had accumulated so many academic degrees I felt like "Father Fahrenheit." However, as I entered St. Thomas Hospital in Akron, Ohio, to serve as chaplain for a short time, a startling thought occurred to me. I had never seen anyone die. I had never seen anyone born. Scenes of suffering and raw grief had all been quarantined out of my academic existence. I somehow sensed that St. Thomas Hospital would be an initiation into areas of life I had never previously entered. I would experience the loves and the hurts, the joys and the sorrows of human existence as never before.

How right I was in my anticipation. In my first week I looked on the corpse of a nineteen-year-old boy who died in a fiery wreckage when his car was struck by a train. I prayed over the body of a twenty-year-old girl who had put a gun in her mouth and sent a bullet searing through her brain. I remember standing over her corpse, studying the dark rings under her closed eyes, and asking: "Why? Why did you do it?" When the morgue attendant brought in the nearest of kin to identify the dead girl, that nearest of kin shrugged disgustedly. "Yeah, that's her," he said. I looked back at the closed eyes and the dark rings of sleeplessness and felt that I understood a little more of the despair that preferred dying to living.

But the most educational of all the experiences was the birth of a baby boy. A retired nursing Sister, who took pity on my inexperience and who took charge of my hospital-life education, told me

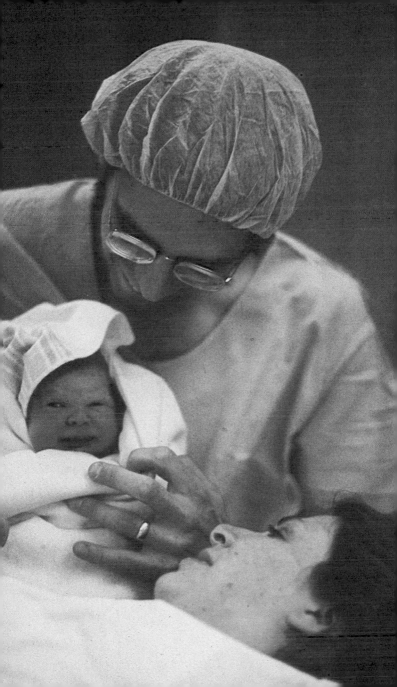

that, before leaving the hospital, I had to see a delivery. Can you believe that I actually asked: "A delivery of what?" The dear Sister replied: "Oh Fella, you're worse off than I thought. You have to see the delivery of a *baby!*"

I warned her that she was apparently wearing her wimple too tight, and that it would alarm the delivering mother if a chaplain were brought in to witness the birth of her child. I also rehearsed a litany of other reasons why this would be imprudent if not impossible, but she saw through them and through me. The next morning I was in the delivery room. The atmosphere was casual and chatty until the actual moment of delivery. Then the room became very still . . . until a baby boy came wriggling into the world. A doctor cleared the baby's breathing passages of mucus with suction tubes and briskly rubbed his chest and back. Then it happened. The baby cried.

When I heard that first wail of life, something very profound happened to me. It had never happened on any of the other momentous occasions of my life, not even on the day of my ordination to the priesthood. I simply turned numb. The doctor, who had been explaining the delivery procedure to me, continued his descriptions, but I didn't really hear. I was utterly overwhelmed by the beauty and sacredness of that moment and what I was seeing.

It was as if my mind were saying, "Cannot compute! Cannot compute!" What I was witnessing was too big, too beautiful, too sacred to fit easily into my mind. My mental machinery simply short-circuited. In a daze I stumbled out of the delivery room, and as I walked down the long corridor of the hospital, my theological education began to connect to what I had just experienced. In the Judeo-Christian tradition, God does not come to know you and me at conception or birth. God does not get such new ideas, nor does he lose old ones. He has known and loved each of us from all eternity.

God had waited from all eternity for that moment of birth. And now he would show his little boy the adoring face of the mother that had carried him so lovingly. He would show that little boy the magnificent stars he had strung in the sky. He would introduce him to the music of lullabies and the softness of his mother's arms, the gentleness of his father's hands. The "I" of God had been saying to the "Thou" of that small baby: "With an everlasting love I have loved you. This is why with loving kindness I created you" (from the prophecy of Jeremiah, 31:3). Cannot compute. Cannot compute. The miracle of life. The Good News of God's love for his world and for each of us. Every new child is a sign that God wants the world to go on.

After my term of service at the hospital, I sorted through all the profoundly human experiences that had been mine. I found that people die as they have lived: afraid or angry, believing or despairing. The human condition with all its superficial foibles and throbbing needs. Goodness mixed with evil. Evil softened by goodness. But the mountaintop experience was certainly the birth of that baby boy. In the long and arduous process of my own psychosexual maturation, it was an undeniable milestone. I understood in that tremendous and insightful experience the miracle of human reproduction. Theologically I felt as though I had touched the smiling face of God, who had lovingly dreamed of that little boy from all eternity and who had conferred upon him the inestimable gift of life.

That child was indeed a unique and unrepeatable image and likeness of God himself. God does not make carbon copies. In the whole history of the human race that little boy had never occurred before, and in the entire course of human history still to be, he will never occur again. No one has ever had or will ever have his fingerprints, his unique combination of gifts, his immortal soul. It is a realization that can enter the mind only gradually. It is a mystery of love that we can only dimly appreciate and never fully understand.

The Death Camp at Dachau: "Never Again"

Some time after the Akron experience I went to Europe for further studies. As all good scholars must, I spent some time in Germany, at the well-known Goethe Institute, trying to deepen my knowledge of the German language. On one of the school tours, we took a trip to Dachau. In that small city stand the remains of one of the Nazi death camps built during Hitler's regime. The German guide who met us there dispassionately told us that the West German government keeps up the death camp as a memorial. It is dedicated to the anonymous millions of human beings who died in these camps. The purpose of a memorial is to help us keep something in mind. Those who do not remember history are doomed to repeat its failures. The guide explained that this stark reminder was kept before the eyes of the world "so that what happened here would *never again* be repeated in the course of human history." The words *Never Again* were on plaques at the gates of Dachau, in five languages.

As our guide escorted us through the barracks where the huddled masses of humanity were imprisoned, I began to have an eerie feeling of unrealness. Did all this really happen? Could human beings really do this to one another? The evidence was before my eyes, but my mind balked at understanding. Finally the guide took us through an oblong extermination building. He explained the "plan" of Dachau. "In this first room, you will notice the clothes hooks. The prisoners of Dachau would be invited to come in here for a warm shower, while their lice-ridden clothes could be deloused. After stripping and hanging up their clothes here in this room, they would be invited into the next room." Our silent group of tourists followed the guide, who continued his explanation with an objectivity which was almost unbelievable. This apparent shower room, with waterless shower heads in the ceiling and open drains in the floor, is actually a gas chamber. "This is where the prisoners were to die." I think all of us felt the shock of deceit, the lingering shadows of death. We were then ushered into the next room of the oblong extermination building. "The corpses were to be stacked here, while a guard with pliers pulled out the reusable gold and silver from the mouths of the dead."

And then into the last room, the room with the ovens where the corpses were to be cremated. The heavily rusted slides were pulled out like slabs waiting for new bodies to be dumped into the flames. The guide explained that around the death camps where these cremations took place, the odor of burned flesh could be detected for five or six miles.

For the second time in my life, I turned numb. If the birth of that baby boy in Akron had been too big, too beautiful, too sacred to fit easily and quickly into my mind, this was too violent and shattering. As the group moved on, I stood there frozen with disbelief. It was as if I were standing in the pit of a nightmare and hoping that I would wake up and find that it had all been a bad dream. The guide gently took my arm and told us we were to go out to view the "Blood Ditch." Soon we were looking at a cement wall, pockmarked by bullets. "The blood of those shot here would drain along these troughs and into this ditch." The Germans had planted red flowers in the troughs and ditch.

The Aching Question

I remember my last look back at the gates of Dachau and the words in so many languages: *Never Again.* I remember saying a prayer, as we left, that such a horrible human tragedy would "never again" be a part of our human history. But back in the mainstream of German life, back on the busy streets of Bavaria, I discovered a question struggling to the surface of my mind. I wanted desperately to ask the German people I met but somehow I couldn't. It sounded too self-righteous, too much like the "Ugly American." The people in Europe had too often endured such embarrassment.

In the movie *Judgment at Nuremberg,* the presiding American judge (played by Spencer Tracy) asks the very question of a middle-aged German couple. It was the question that writhed in me: "Did you know?" he asked. The wife offered a volley of obscurities about the benefits that Hitler had brought to Germany: the jobs, the new prosperity, the autobahn. "Of these other things," she added, "we knew nothing." However, when her husband began to describe how well the Gestapo was organized, how resistance endangered one's very life, he clearly implied that, of course, they did know. (How could you hear the sirens, see the vans, and watch the human cargo being carted away, how could you hear the gunshots and smell the burning flesh . . . and not know?) The judge remarked: "But your wife just said you didn't know." Both husband and wife silently looked down. Their bowed heads were saying: "Yes, we did know."

I have a great love and admiration for the German people. I certainly don't want to pose as accuser and judge. I have no delusions about my own courage. Time and circumstance have mercifully separated me and spared me from the call to join the Hitler Youth, to wear an SS uniform, or even to turn my eyes away from mass murder on the pretense of being an innocent bystander.

I know the fate of Dietrich Bonhoeffer who spurned "cheap grace" and paid the price of his life for a "costly discipleship." I know the fate of my own Jesuit brother, Alfred Delp, who wrote his last words in the concentration camp (*Im Angesicht des Todes—Prison Meditations of Father Delp*). I know the fate of these and other brave Christians and Jews who spoke out. I know that I could easily have been involved in this drama of life and death. I know that I must not too readily identify myself with the hero-victims. I know that it is much easier to express outrage than to stand up bravely against the persuasive power of a pointed gun.

Our guide at Dachau had given each of us a booklet. The words exposed rather than obscured the truth. I will always admire this German honesty and contrition. The pictures told a grisly story of staring corpses, the piles of shoes, the scratched and bloody walls of the gas chambers, the blackened smokestacks of Auschwitz, Treblinka, Buchenwald, and Dachau. "Never Again!"

Death Comes to the Convent Children

By the end of my course at the Goethe Institute, my German was fairly fluent. So I became a summer chaplain to a convent of Sisters in the village of Flittard, outside Cologne. One of the older Sisters, "Schwester Rutilia," practiced German conversation with me in the convent garden each afternoon. The spirit of this dear Sister always seemed bent under some hidden burden. I presumed for a while that it was my German. Then on a particularly sunny afternoon, the spirit moved me and I plunged right into the question: "Sister, is there some deep pain inside you? Do you want to talk about it? I listen very well in German."

The dear Sister poured out to me a heartful of sorrows. She explained that she and her Sisters at one time provided a home for retarded and handicapped children. The Sisters in Sister Rutilia's religious order had been trained to take care of

these children and loved them "as if they were our own children."

> Then one day we heard that the government was planning to take them away and to kill them, just because they were retarded or handicapped. At first we could not believe this, but we prayed anyway. Oh, how we prayed for our children! But one day the vans came and soldiers took away our little babies. They threw them into the vans like sacks of potatoes and took them off to the "killing centers." They said that they were killed because they couldn't make a contribution to the Third Reich. They were only an expense, a burden.

Then Sister Rutilia told me the shocking facts which I later investigated and confirmed for myself. She explained that in the early 1930s, a determined group of opinion makers in Germany propagandized a new ethic, the pragmatic morality of Hegel, the German philosopher. In summary, this ethic maintains: Whatever solves a problem on the practical level must be considered as moral. No action is right or wrong in itself. If a given action results in a desirable effect, it is ethically acceptable. Simply put, the end justifies the means. Sister Rutilia continued:

> Even before Hitler came into power, this philosophy was heavily propagandized and generally accepted in Germany. The educational and the judicial systems began to lean in this direction. When Hitler could no longer be successfully or openly opposed, he set up the "killing centers." He ordered the deaths of the insane, the aged in state homes, the retarded, and the deformed. Their crime was that they could not contribute. They were a burden and expense. They were not wanted, and because they were not wanted— they were killed.

I mentioned that I had to confirm this for myself. It seemed so coldly subhuman, like a sudden plunge from civilization into savagery. According to the Sister, and confirmed in my own subsequent research, at least a quarter million Gentile lives were taken because they were deemed "not meaningful or productive." With all this blood on his hands, Hitler felt empowered to announce: "And now we must undertake the final solution of the Jewish problem." Hitler promised that the mass slaughter of Jews would release the vast amounts of money they controlled into the German economy. It would be a step toward the emergence of the Aryan (non-Jewish Caucasian) Super Race. The principle had been officially established: "Whoever is not wanted must die." They (the Jews) are not wanted. Therefore they must die. It was the airtight logic of the Hegelian ethic.

It is an ominous and frightening feeling to sense the direction in which our own country is moving only fifty years later. It is so true that those who do not remember human failures in history are doomed to repeat them. Ethically we seem to be where Germany was in 1930. It is the best of times; it is the worst of times. It is for us now a time of crisis, a time for a national clarification of moral values. The camps are formed. The judicial system and the media are leaning clearly toward the Hegelian ethic. The rhetorical confrontation has begun. The question is the value and sacredness of human life. Syndicated writer Nick Thimmesch says that the only difference is that we can protest without being arrested by the Gestapo. In a *Newsweek* article dated July 9, 1973, he writes:

> The extremes of the utilitarian mentality rampaging today through medicine, the drug industry and

government will be checked by our press, lawmakers and doctors, lawyers and clergymen holding to the traditional ethic. The Germans weren't blessed that way.

The Confirmation by Doctor Alexander

In 1946 and 1947 Dr. Leo Alexander, a Boston psychiatrist, was a consultant to the Secretary of War and on duty with the Office of Chief of Counsel for War Crimes in Nuremberg. After two years of scholarly probing into the Nazi nightmare, which Alexander sees as an outgrowth of the acceptance of Hegelian morality, Dr. Alexander published a remarkable article in *The New England Journal of Medicine,* under date of July 14, 1949.

Dr. Alexander entitled his article "Medical Practice Under Dictatorship." In this article the doctor confirms in technical language what Sister Rutilia told me in the convent garden at Flittard.

According to Dr. Alexander, the seeds of human destruction in Germany were planted in the growing acceptance of the Hegelian pragmatic morality: If it provides a solution for a practical problem, it is morally justifiable. The (desirable) end justifies the (evil) means. The trend toward this morality, increasingly evident in our own country at this time, began in Germany even before Hitler came into power in 1933. Dr. Alexander writes that the deluge of propaganda to rationalize killing on the grounds of usefulness began even before Hitler's rise to power.

> . . . a propaganda barrage was directed against the traditional compassionate, nineteenth-century attitudes toward the chronically ill, and for the adoption

of a utilitarian, Hegelian point of view. Sterilization and euthanasia of persons with chronic mental illnesses was [*sic*] discussed at a meeting of Bavarian psychiatrists in 1931. [p. 39]

When Hitler did come into unopposed domination, the Hegelian morality of "rational utility" replaced "moral, ethical, and religious values." Medical science in Nazi Germany willingly collaborated. Many doctors who had taken a Hippocratic oath to preserve life became the social executioners of the Third Reich. Francis Schaeffer and C. Everett Koop, M.D., in their book *Whatever Happened to the Human Race?* (Revell, 1979), comment:

> The first to be killed were the aged, the infirm, the senile and mentally retarded, and defective children. Eventually, as World War II approached, the doomed undesirables included epileptics, World War I amputees, children with badly modeled ears, and even bed wetters. Physicians took part in this planning on matters of life and death to save society's money. [p. 106]

In *Judgment at Nuremberg*, the condemned German said, "But we didn't think it would go that far."

The American answered, "It went that far the very first time you condemned an innocent human being."

CHAPTER 3

THE NAZI NIGHTMARE
IN THE AMERICAN DREAM

"In Germany
they first came for the Communists,
and I didn't speak up because I wasn't
a Communist.
Then they came for the Jews,
and I didn't speak up because I wasn't
a Jew.
Then they came for the Trade Unionists,
and I didn't speak up because I wasn't
a Trade Unionist.
Then they came for the Catholics,
and I didn't speak up because I was
a Protestant.
Then they came for me . . . and by that time
there was no one left to speak up."
—Pastor Martin Neimoller

The "Killing Centers"

Dr. Alexander's research revealed that there was a "mass extermination of the chronically sick in the interest of saving 'useless' expenses to the community as a whole" (p. 39). This extermination took place at "killing centers." By an order from Hitler on September 1, 1939, questionnaires were filled out on all patients in state institutions. Which patients were to be killed was determined by a board of doctors, most of whom were professors of psychiatry in key German universities. These doctors processed more than one thousand questionnaires a week and stamped most of them: "Death!" The doctors never saw any of the patients themselves. They looked only at medical charts. The victims "included the mentally defective, psychotics (particularly schizophrenics), epileptics and patients suffering from infirmities of old age and from various organic neurologic disorders such as infantile paralysis [polio], Parkinsonism, multiple sclerosis and brain tumors" (p. 40). Also marked for death were people who were suffering from "simple depressions, involutional depressions."

These questionnaires, which became the prescriptions for death for so many of the sick and disabled, were conducted and collected by the "Realm's Work Committee of Institutions for Cure and Care." Dr. Alexander adds that a parallel organization devoted exclusively to the killing of children was known by the similarly euphemistic name of the "Realm's Committee for Scientific Approach to Severe Illness Due to Heredity and Constitution." These were the names of the groups who processed the questionnaires. Dr. Alexander also identifies the "Charitable Transport Company for the Sick" as the agency that transported patients to the "killing centers."

Ironically there was still another agency, called the "Charitable Foundation for Institutional Care," which collected the cost of the killings from the families and relatives of the victims. Of course, these people were never truthfully informed about the reason for these charges. On the death certificates the cause of death was always falsified. According to the German records, 275,000 people were put to death in these "killing centers." However, this was only the beginning. As Dr. Alexander says, "This program was merely the entering wedge for exterminations of far greater scope" (p. 40).

There were many experiments in killing conducted at these "killing centers." Dr. Alexander calls it "the science of annihilation" and says that "a large part of this research was devoted to the science of destroying and preventing [through sterilization] life, for which I have proposed the term 'ktenology,' the science of killing" (p. 41).

Medical Experimentation

There was considerable experimentation done on those people docketed for death, such as amputations and gunshots into the spleen in order to test blood coagulants. There were live dissections to show the effects of explosive decompression. At Dachau, where most of the prisoners were Polish priests, three hundred prisoners were immersed in freezing water; eighty to ninety of them died as a result. According to Dr. Alexander, the experimentation of Dr. Sigmund Rascher ultimately revealed that "it actually took from eighty minutes to five or six hours to kill an undressed person in such a manner, whereas a man in full aviator's dress took six or seven hours to kill" (p. 43). There was also considerable testing by injection with strains of bacteria and viruses. During one period of experimentation a group of gypsies was given only camouflaged seawater to drink and "suffered the tortures of the damned."

Dutch Resistance to the "Fatal First Step"

It should be noted that when the Reich Commander for the Occupied Netherlands Territories invited Dutch physicians to rehabilitate people for the sole purpose of putting them to forced labor, the Dutch doctors adamantly refused. They knew it would be the first, slight step away from principle and medical ethics. They were men in the service of men. They would not treat human beings like pawns. When these Dutch physicians were threatened with revocation of their licenses, they simply mailed in their licenses and took down their shingles. Even when the Reich Commander had one hundred Dutch doctors arrested and sent to concentration camps, the whole Dutch medical profession continued to stand firm. They took care of their patients quietly and privately, but they would not give in. Dr. Alexander marvels that because of this, not a single killing or sterilization "was recommended or participated in by any Dutch physician."

In his article, Dr. Alexander clearly identifies the "fatal first step," the corrosion that begins in microscopic proportions. In the end it became a nightmare of savagery, the bloody conclusion of Hegelian rational utility and pragmatic morality. But it all begins with one assumption:

> It started with the acceptance of the attitude basic in the euthanasia movement, that there is such a thing as a life not worthy to be lived. [p. 44]

Commenting on this statement of Dr. Alexander, Francis Schaeffer and Dr. C. Everett Koop add: "That is exactly what is being accepted today in the abortion, infanticide, and euthanasia movements." It is the "fatal first step," the lethal assumption that can move a country from a compassionate, humanitarian ethic to a merciless ethic which forbids any human being to be a burden under penalty of death.

America at the Crossroads

As far back as 1949, when Leo Alexander wrote his article, he could foresee America and American doctors standing at the brink of "Hegelian utilitarianism." He saw even then among American doctors "a certain amount of rather open contempt for the people who cannot be rehabilitated with present knowledge" (p. 45). Dr. Alexander suggested that the "rationalistic point of view has insidiously crept into the motivation of medical effort, supplanting the old Hippocratic point of view" (p. 46). He continues:

> It is natural in such a setting [a dictatorship] that eventually Hegel's principle that "what is useful is good" wins out completely. The killing center is the *reductio ad absurdum* of all health planning based only on rational principles and economy and not on

humane compassion and divine law. To be sure, American physicians are still far from the point of thinking of killing centers, but they have arrived at a danger point in thinking, at which likelihood of full rehabilitation is considered a factor that should determine the amount of time, effort and cost to be devoted to a particular type of patient on the part of the social body upon which this decision rests. At this point Americans should remember that the enormity of a euthanasia movement is present in their own midst. . . .

The case, therefore, that I should like to make is that American medicine must realize where it stands in its fundamental premises. There can be no doubt that in a subtle way the Hegelian premise of "what is useful is right" has infected society, including the medical portion. Physicians must return to the older premises, which were the emotional foundation and driving force of an amazingly successful quest to increase powers of healing and which are bound to carry them still farther if they are not held down to earth by the pernicious attitudes of an overdone practical realism.

What occurred in Germany may have been the inexorable historical progression that the Greek historians have described as the law of the fall of civilizations and that Toynbee has convincingly confirmed—namely, that there is a logical sequence from Koros to Hybris to Ate, which means from surfeit to disdainful arrogance to disaster, the surfeit being increased scientific and practical accomplishments, which, however, brought about an inclination to throw away the old motivations and values by disdainful arrogant pride in practical efficiency. Moral and physical disaster is the inevitable consequence. [p. 46]

Personal Responsibility

I thank you for your patience in reliving with me

35

my own memories and the nightmare of Nazi Germany. I have gone into this frightening chapter of human history because it is such an integral part of my own story and part of the basis of my fears for our own country. I am convinced that we are in the process of writing a similar, nightmarish chapter in our own American history. My heart experiences the loneliness of a prophet-not-listened-to. My inner sense of emergency cries out at the brink of an American tragedy: Is anyone there? Does anyone see what I see? Does anyone care?

In an article published in the *Christian Crusade Weekly* (1979), Columnist Dan Lyons writes:

> At Nuremberg, Hitler and his henchmen were condemned by the American judges because they encouraged the killing of the unborn. . . . Hitler was wrong, even though most of the men on our Supreme Court today defend what the Nazis did. If we do not stop killing infants on the premise that they are nothing unless they weigh five or six pounds, we will do what Hitler did: we will kill the handicapped, particularly when those handicapped are aged. Then we will kill the truly handicapped who are retarded: the only "angels" among us, for they have never sinned. . . . Unless we stop abortion we will go further than Hitler, being "better" educated than the Austrian paperhanger. We will kill infants after they are born. We will do it scientifically, of course. . . . We will call on brilliant scientists who know all about creation. . . . We will ask them to tell us which child is worthy to live and which is not. We will go Hitler one better. We will commit wholesale infanticide, like pagan Rome, where even healthy infants were often put to death if they were not masculine, like their executioners. There is no doubt scientists will cooperate, as they did for Hitler. We already have many of them clamoring for the death of the elderly and the "unfit."

In an article entitled "No-Fault Guilt-Free History" (*New York Times*, Feb. 16, 1976), Dr. Richard M. Hunt, associate dean of Harvard University's Graduate School of Arts and Science, describes the reaction of his students to a course which he calls "Moral Dilemma in a Repressive Society: Nazi Germany." About their end-of-term papers, Dr. Hunt notes that the most disturbing feature of these papers was the rationalization by his students of personal responsibility. Dr. Hunt writes:

> Clearly some trends of our times seem to be running towards a no-fault, that is, a guilt-free society. One might say that the virtues of responsible choice, paying the penalty, taking the consequences, all appear at low ebb today.

> Somehow, I have got to convey the meaning of moral decisions and their relation to significant outcomes. Most important, I want to point out that single acts of individuals and strong stands of institutions at an early date do make a difference in the long run. I am through with teaching no-fault history.

American psychiatrist Dr. Frederic Wertham, in his book *A Sign for Cain: An Exploration of Human Violence* (Macmillan, 1966), makes a convincing case for the fact that the people of Germany were not evil or fanatical. The process of societal rationalization of evil is a gradual, cooperative process. It relieves the individual of the burdens of personal morality and responsibility. Dr. Wertham suggests that the German people surrendered their individual responsibility and conscience to the State. The doctors, he suggests, who carried out the killings in various human extermination programs were not madmen. They had simply brought the Hegelian line of utilitarianism to its logical conclusion. They were concerned about the financial cost of caring for a patient in contrast to the cheap solution of killing that patient.

I think that America is rushing along the same depersonalizing and dehumanizing course. I think that the major milestone in that path which moves from civilization to savagery occurred on January 22, 1973. The outrageous decision of the United States Supreme Court to legalize abortion-on-demand has opened the floodgates of death and released the fury. The terrible indifference toward human life in that decision, and especially the language of Justice Blackmun about a "meaningful life," would seem to make all the other forms of killing simple logical corollaries.

In his *Newsweek* article, previously quoted, Nick Thimmesch writes:

> The utilitarian ethic is also common in the arguments of euthanasia advocates at work in six state legislatures. Their euphemisms drip like honey (should say, cyanide?) just as they did in Germany—"death with dignity," the "good death." Their legal arguments fog the mind. Their mentality shakes me. . . . It bothers me that eugenicists in Germany organized the mass destruction of mental patients, and in the United States pro-abortionists now also serve in pro-euthanasia organizations. Sorry, but I see a pattern.

"NEVER AGAIN!" . . .
"YES, AGAIN!"

"We have paid some high prices for the technological conquest of nature, but none perhaps so high as the intellectual and spiritual costs of seeing nature as mere material for our manipulation, exploitation and transformation. With the powers for biological engineering now gathering, there will be splendid new opportunities for a similar degradation in our view of man. Indeed, we are already witnessing the erosion of our idea of man as something splendid or divine, as a creature with freedom and dignity. And clearly, if we come to see ourselves as meat, then meat we shall become."

—Dr. Leon R. Kass, Professor of the
   Liberal Arts of Human Biology,
   University of Chicago, from
   "Making Babies—The New Biology
   and the 'Old' Morality" in
   The Public Interest (Winter, 1972, p. 53)

Forty Years After Hitler: Yes, Again!

In 1960 I had completed my doctoral studies and returned from Europe. My first assignment was to teach future priests in the Jesuit theologate. In those first years back, I delighted in recalling the years in Europe, and in regaling others with stories of people met and places seen. I never talked about Dachau, or what I learned from Sister Rutilia and found confirmed by Dr. Alexander. It was a sensitive and fearful memory. It was an exposed nerve that I could not touch without profound pain. If the birth of that baby boy in Akron was too big, too beautiful, and too sacred to absorb quickly, the ovens of Dachau, the tears of Rutilia, and the warnings of Dr. Alexander told a story that was too violent, too shocking for immediate realization. The painful history of Nazi Germany was an actual history that somehow in retrospect seemed more like fiction. It was a memory that would not surface easily but would not fade away. It offered its only comfort in the words of hope on the gates at Dachau: *Never Again!*

Then came January 22, 1973. New York State, under the strongly pro-abortion governor, Nelson Rockefeller, had been the harbinger, the wedge of evil. Now the Supreme Court had nationalized the tragedy. It signaled a new "slaughter of the innocents," as one commentator put it. Since that moment my mind has reeled at the proliferation of death-on-demand. I carry the same pain in my heart that I found in the heart of Sister Rutilia in the garden of Flittard outside Cologne.

All the consolation of "Never Again" was gone

in the shattering announcement. There is still something in me that wants to wake up and find that it has all been a bad dream. But the television, newspapers, and newsmagazines constantly confirm what my ears do not want to hear and my heart dreads. Legalized abortion is a new fact of American life.

During the years since 1973 there has been a side of my life filled with brightness. I have been a successful teacher, a popular author, in demand as a public speaker. The dark underside was always the ever-present sadness of proliferating abortions, the triumph of the new ethic of usefulness; and this brought into my life a new dejection, a new loneliness, and even occasional insomnia—all new wrinkles. The announced statistics were horrifying. There were mounting propaganda efforts of the pro-abortion forces, glowing in their newly won legal triumphs. There were pages of advertisements in one of the Chicago newspapers, prior to an exposé of the butchery in abortion clinics. The abortion mills—a name which seems much more accurate than "clinics," the name for places where people are cured—put up their signs everywhere. It was big business getting ever bigger. Euphemistic language and societal rationalization were hiding the stark and bloody realities of the American "killing centers."

Doctor Kelly—Physician and Prophet

My own inner struggles found public expression in the gesture of a Chicago physician, Dr. John Kelly. He simply left this country. He asked publicly the painful question that had ached inside me since Dachau: How does one pretend to be an innocent bystander at a mass murder? How does one in good conscience pay tax monies, knowing that some of that money will be used to finance killing? In leaving the country, Dr. Kelly predicted that, in the wake of the Supreme Court decision to legalize abortion, there would be waves of new propaganda arguing for all forms of killing, just as there had been in Germany. The Nazi drama was being reenacted on an American stage, in the land of the free and the home of the brave.

Malcolm Muggeridge, in an article in the *Human Life Review* (Fall, 1977), called the legalization of abortion a "slippery slope." The Supreme Court has offered the Hegelian ethic its own legal blessing to help rationalize the taking of unborn lives, but the logical extensions of this Hegelian principle are obvious. It is only a matter of time, as Dr. Kelly foresaw, when death-on-demand would completely shatter the ethics of compassion and the ideal of unconditional love in this country. When the value and sacredness of every human life were publicly forsaken in that Supreme Court decision, the walls of civilization began to crumble around us. The door has been opened; the disastrous results are inevitable. Please read on and see what you think. Tell me if the opinions and the events chronicled here are not simply a rerun of the Nazi nightmare.

Death-on-Demand in America

- In May, 1973, four months after the Supreme Court decision, Dr. James D. Watson, a Nobel Prize Laureate, granted an interview to *Prism* magazine, at that time a publication of the American Medical Association. *Time* magazine, in its May 28, 1973, issue, made the interview public and quoted Watson as saying: "If a child were not declared alive until three days after birth, then all parents could be allowed the choice that only a few are given under the present system. The doctor could allow the child to die if the parents so chose and save a lot of misery and suffering." (p. 104)

- In January, 1978, another Nobel Laureate, Dr. Francis Crick, was quoted in the *Pacific News Service* as follows: "no newborn infant should be declared human until it has passed certain tests regarding its genetic endowment and that if it fails these tests it forfeits the right to live." (Crick has also proposed compulsory death for everyone at age eighty.)

- In the prestigious *New England Journal of Medicine,* in October of 1973, nine months after the Supreme Court decision, Drs. Raymond S. Duff and A. G. M. Campbell of the Yale University Medical School published a paper openly advocating the option of death for defective infants. They suggest in the article that most parents of babies suffering handicaps cannot come to the physician and say, "My baby has a life not worthy to be lived." The doctors maintain that such parents are not in a condition to give "informed" consent to the death of their child. So the doctors propose that the parents need help from the physician to do so. The doctors propose that all management options must be presented to the parents and death is one of the

options in the treatment of a defective new-born. (It is, of course, the "fatal first step" to which Dr. Leo Alexander refers, in which it is assumed "that there is such a thing as a life not worthy to be lived." If this judgment and death decision can be made for infants, why not for anyone who is handicapped or senile?)

- The *Newsweek* magazine for November 12, 1973, in reporting on the Duff and Campbell article, quotes Duff as saying: "The public has got to decide what to do with vegetated individuals who have no human potential." A letter of response to *Newsweek*, published three weeks after the article appeared, seems worthy of reproduction.

"LIFE-AND-DEATH DECISIONS"

"I'll wager my entire root system and as much fertilizer as it would take to fill Yale University that you have never received a letter from a vegetable before this one, but, much as I resent the term, I must confess that I fit the description of a 'vegetable' as defined in the article 'Shall This Child Die?'

"Due to severe brain damage incurred at birth, I am unable to dress myself, toilet myself, or write; my secretary is typing this letter. Many thousands of dollars had to be spent on my rehabilitation and education in order for me to reach my present professional status as a counseling psychologist. My parents were also told, 35 years ago, that there was 'little or no hope of achieving meaningful "humanhood"' for their daughter. Have I reached 'humanhood'? Compared with Drs. Duff and Campbell, I believe I have surpassed it!

"Instead of changing the law to make it legal to weed out us 'vegetables,' let us change the laws so that we may receive quality medical care, education and freedom to live as full and productive lives as our potentials allow."

—Sondra Diamond,
Philadelphia, Pa.

● Dr. William Gaylin, a professor of psychiatry and law at Columbia University, told a conference of the American Association of University Women: "It used to be easy to know what we wanted for our children, and now the best for our children might mean deciding which ones to kill. We've always wanted the best for our grandparents, and now that might mean killing them."

● In 1975, The Sonoma (California) Conference on Ethical Issues in Neonatal Intensive Care published a 193-page report entitled "Ethics of Newborn Intensive Care." During the conference, it was reported, a panel of twenty people in the health care field was asked this question: "Would it be right to directly intervene to kill a [severely defective though] self-sustaining infant?" (Note: A self-sustaining infant is one who can live without technical assistance of any kind. This baby can survive with no help other than normal feeding.) Seventeen of the twenty panelists agreed that such direct intervention would be a permissible option. They answered yes to the question. It is sadly interesting to note that the three physicians on the panel said that they would hesitate to kill such a self-sustaining infant directly, but would not prevent someone else from doing the killing.

● Dr. R. T. F. Schmidt, at that time president-elect of the American College of Obstetrics and

Gynecologists, when asked about the consensus of the Sonoma Conference, had this to say: "The fact that seventeen of twenty expert panelists believe that some severely defective infants should be killed under certain conditions is not only deeply disturbing to our traditional concept of the inherent value of human life but is potentially shattering to the foundations of Western civilization." (*Pediatric News*, April, 1977, p. 30)

- A recent article in a prestigious medical journal proposed that medical experimentation should be done on children with Down's syndrome (mongolism) because such children make no other contribution to society.

- Dr. Joseph Fletcher, in an article in the *American Journal of Nursing* (73:670 [1973]), said that it was ridiculous to give ethical approval to ending a "subhuman" life by abortion but refuse to give that same approval to ending a "subhuman" life by positive euthanasia (actively killing a terminally ill or mentally defective person). Dr. Fletcher has been one of the major proponents and popularizers of "situation ethics," a system which in general denies the existence of absolute values.

- In 1976, a bill (#1207) was proposed to the Wisconsin state legislature allowing any resident of the state of Wisconsin to request and empower another to kill him/her. The person who does the killing, according to the proposal, must be fourteen years of age or older. The death request may be written or oral. The person who does the killing will not be guilty of murder, manslaughter, or homicide. Persons under eighteen who thus request death will have to notify their parents or guardian prior to making a valid death request, but parents cannot forbid the killing.

- A Swedish public health physician, Dr. Ragnar Toss, wants to open a suicide clinic, "not to treat them, but to help them do it." Dr. Toss says that his suggestion is a logical outgrowth of the choice that women now have about abortions. (*Swedish Medical Journal*, Aug., 1977)

- A British doctor, John Goundry, says that a "death pill will be available and in all likelihood will be obligatory by the end of this century." He adds, "In the end I can see the state taking over and insisting on euthanasia." (*Philadelphia Evening Bulletin*, Aug. 13, 1977)

- Philip Handler, president of the prestigious U.S. National Academy of Science, has said that the time has come to exert a national policy of eliminating defective unborn babies.

- A Yale University geneticist, Dr. Y. Edward Hsia, speaking at the annual meeting of the American Association for the Advancement of Science in December, 1972, suggested mandatory prenatal tests to discover defective unborn babies and, in such cases, compulsory death for the defective by abortion.

- Psychiatrist Florence Clothier, addressing the First Euthanasia Conference in 1968, said, "We . . . would want to include death of the body for those whose central nervous system and mind

49

are already dead. . . . What clock that can tick but cannot tell time is preserved and cherished at prohibitive costs, financial and emotional?"

- In his book *Ideals of Life* (Wiley, 1954), Millard S. Everett, professor of philosophy at Oklahoma A & M, suggests that "when public opinion is ready for it" no child should be allowed to live "who would be certain to suffer social handicap."

- In the United States it is statistically confirmed that the most dangerous place for anyone to be, with regard to the preservation of one's life, is in the womb of one's mother.

The Cases of Doctors Edelin, Floyd, and Waddill

- In January of 1975, Dr. Kenneth Edelin, chief resident in obstetrics and gynecology at Boston City Hospital, went on trial for manslaughter. The age of the unborn child, killed by Dr. Edelin, was estimated to be approximately twenty-four weeks (six months). Dr. Edelin decided to kill the baby by a saline abortion. A strong solution was pumped into the amniotic sac on three separate occasions but had failed to scald the baby to death, as such fluid usually does. Babies aborted in this manner are the so-called "candied apple babies" because the outer layer of skin, the epidermis, is completely burned by the caustic solution injected by the doctor. Finally Dr. Edelin decided on an "abortion by hysterotomy." According to an assistant at the operation, Dr. Edelin made the incision, then reached in to suffocate the baby by disconnecting the baby's placenta from the womb.

The assistant doctor said that Dr. Edelin kept his hand in the womb for three minutes by the clock on the wall. Ordinarily three minutes would insure suffocation. The baby would get no oxygen from within or from without. After three minutes, Dr. Edelin took the baby out. He felt the little boy's chest for three to five seconds and noticed no heart beat. He presumed that the child was dead. He placed the body in a stainless steel basin held by a nurse. She deposited it into a container in the back room. According to medical experts, in examination of the baby's lungs, there was clear evidence that the baby had been born alive. It was concluded that the baby had died somewhere between the abortion chamber and the morgue where the body was taken.

The judge in the Edelin case instructed the jury that the Supreme Court had legalized abortion for the entire term of pregnancy, and that, according to the same Supreme Court, a person (someone who has rights and the protection of the law) exists only after birth. By his instructions to the jury, the judge decided that the jury could convict Dr. Edelin only if they were sure that he had caused the death of the baby after he had been born. If death resulted from something Dr. Edelin had done before the baby was taken from his mother's body, the jury could not convict Dr. Edelin. The jury in fact returned a verdict of manslaughter. The judge imposed a sentence of probation only. The Supreme Judicial Court of Massachusetts a short time later fully absolved Edelin of all guilt.

Law professor John T. Noonan, Jr., in his outstanding book *A Private Choice: Abortion in America in the Seventies* (Free Press, 1979), says that this case "was a great victory for the pro-abortion party." The liberty to kill living and born babies had almost been reached and legalized in American courts.

- In the summer of 1974, the liberty to kill living and born babies was given further legal sanction in the case of Dr. Jesse T. Floyd, of Columbia, South Carolina. Dr. Floyd aborted what seemed to be a seven-month-old baby. The mother of this child had paid $250 for an abortion, and the abortion was caused by an injection of prostoglandins. The baby boy, marked for death, was born alive and lived for twenty days. He apparently died from injuries that were caused by the prostoglandins. The legal milestone of this case is that the judge, Chief Circuit Judge Clement Haynsworth, held Dr. Floyd innocent without trial. In his judgment, Haynsworth assumed that the baby boy who lived twenty days had not been a viable fetus because he had not lived indefinitely.

- Dr. William B. Waddill, Jr., was indicted in June of 1977 for allegedly strangling to death a baby girl following a saline abortion at the Westminster County Hospital in California. At a preliminary hearing Dr. Ronald Cornelsen testified that Dr. Waddill throttled the infant's neck, strangling her, while complaining of what might happen to him (lawsuits) if the baby were to live. He allegedly discussed drowning the baby or injecting her with a fatal solution. He supposed-

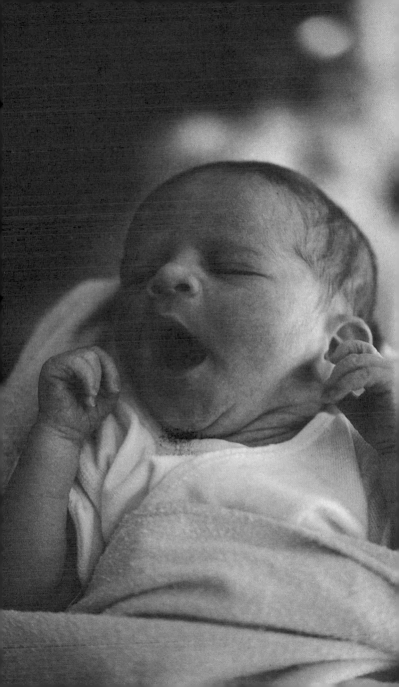

ly complained that the baby just would not die! While the baby was being examined by Dr. Cornelsen, Dr. Waddill, according to the testimony of Dr. Cornelsen, tried again to strangle the baby.

The trial resulted in a hung jury without any conclusion about the supposed strangling because the judge unexplainably introduced new material concerning a California definition of death which really had very little to do with the subject.

In these three cases the legal barriers to infanticide were considerably lowered. All three doctors brought about the death of a living human baby. None was punished by the American judicial system. It is interesting to note that when the jury convicted Dr. Edelin of manslaughter, members of that jury received anonymous death threats. Dr. Edelin appeared on television to restrain those threatening to kill the members of the jury. He said that this was no way to "make our point."

More Proponents of the New Ethic

- Dr. Christian Barnard, the South African surgeon who performed the first heart transplant, campaigns for euthanasia in his recent book *Good Life Good Death: A Doctor's Case for Euthanasia and Suicide* (Prentice-Hall, 1980). He holds that the only reasonable thing for doctors to do for some of their patients is to kill them.

- Dr. Martin Kohl wrote in 1970: "In some situations, especially certain cases of euthanasia, morality demands the killing of the innocent." Three years later, after the Supreme Court decision, "during a 30-month period at Yale-New Haven Hospital's intensive-care nursery, 43 infants were permitted to die because vital treatment was deliberately withheld." (*Newsweek*, Nov. 12, 1973, p. 70)

- Dr. Walter Sackett, a former Florida state legislator, wanted 90 percent of the fifteen hundred mentally retarded patients in Florida hospitals to be allowed to die, under a proposed "Death with Dignity" bill. Dr. Sackett also proposed that children with Down's syndrome should be permitted to succumb to pneumonia. He argued that this strategy would save the state of Florida $5 billion in fifty years.

- In his widely acclaimed book *The Sanctity of Life and the Criminal Law* (Knopf, 1957), Dr. Glanville Williams ends with a plea for the legalization of "humanitarian infanticide" and for "euthanasia for handicapped children."

- In 1974, Dr. Robert Cooke, vice chancellor of medicine at the University of Wisconsin, testified before the Senate Health Subcommittee that an estimated two thousand infants a year are dying in America because treatment is withheld or stopped. (Many doctors think that the number is actually much larger than two thousand.)

- A 1975 Montana bill would allow a doctor to administer euthanasia (called "medicated death"), or order a nurse to do so, or even give lethal drugs to the family for their use.

The New Ethic: Only a Matter of Time?

Is anyone there? Does anyone see what I see? Does anyone care?

Of course, opinions and proposals like the ones cited above could be multiplied endlessly. The basic argument is for a New Ethic that would replace the Old Ethic. The New Ethic assumes that there are lives not worthy to be lived and that these persons ought to be put to death before or after birth; their deaths would relieve others of financial and emotional burdens. The Old Ethic would insist on the *sanctity* and *value* of each human life, and would deny that there is such a thing as a life not worthy to be lived. The New Ethic would judge each life by its *quality* and *meaningfulness* and would put to death those whose lives did not meet the required standards. People should be allowed to live only if they meet certain standards of usefulness and productivity. The message is: We do not want and will not tolerate you if you are a burden, especially a financial or emotional burden, to us. We will let you live only if we judge that you can have a "meaningful, useful, and productive" life. We do not allow defectives.

This New Ethic is, of course, the undisguised usefulness theory of Hegel that rationalized and motivated the conduct of the medical practitioners of Germany's Third Reich. Today in our country the media, the judicial system, and the medical community are leaning, if not pushing, in this direction. The New Ethic proponents feel that total victory is very near. Soon the sensitivities of the general public will be sufficiently desensitized.

People will "get used" to it, and the killing of undesirables, whose lives do not meet the required standards, can proceed without sticky litigation in the courts.

CHAPTER **5** _____

BREAKING THE
UNBEARABLE SILENCE
Discovery and Disbelief

"Throughout the primitive world the doctor
and the sorcerer tended to be the same person. . . . With the Greeks . . . the distinction
[between the healing physician and the killing
sorcerer] was made clear. One profession, the
followers of Asclepius, were to be dedicated
completely to life under all circumstances,
regardless of rank, age, or intellect—the life of
a slave, the life of the Emperor, the life of a
foreign man, the life of a defective child. . . .
This is a priceless possession which we cannot
afford to tarnish, but society always is attempt-
ing to make the physician into a killer—to kill
the defective child at birth, to leave the sleeping pills beside the bed of the cancer patient.
. . . It is the duty of society to protect the
physician from such requests."

> —Margaret Mead, anthropologist,
> from a personal communication (1961)
> quoted in *Psychiatry and Ethics*
> by Maurice Levine, M.D.
> (George Braziller, 1972, pp. 324-25)

Three Young Women

To return to my own story, since January 22, 1973, I have personally carried an increasingly heavy burden of lonely concern. The death-on-demand movement received a great impetus from the Supreme Court, and its proponents have begun leading us more and more boldly and outspokenly into the dehumanized world of the New Ethic. I kept thinking of Akron, Dachau, Sister Rutilia, Leo Alexander, and "Never Again!" At the same time I was painfully aware of the success of the pro-euthanasia forces as the "quality of life" ethic came more and more to replace the "sanctity of life" ethic. The grim statistics were quoted in the newspapers. Celebrities began telling the world of their abortions. Of course the language was always euphemistic. The pro-abortionists and the media spoke only of "terminating a pregnancy." They never mentioned the baby who died in each abortion.

Finally I could no longer live passively with the personal anguish. Like Dr. Kelly, I could no longer pretend to be an innocent bystander at mass murder. Strangely enough it was not the distant beating of the death drums in the media, the courts, and the clinics. It was not the heartbreaking statistics or the new boldness of the death-on-demand propagandists. I knew I had to "do something" because of three young women who came to talk to me.

The first of the three simply blurted out, "I have had an abortion. I killed my baby. Yes, I knew what I was doing. I was a biology major in college. I even asked one of the nurses in the abortion clinic if there was any way to baptize the baby before we killed it. She told me to 'shut up' or I would upset the other women. She reminded me that they were doing me a favor. She said that they didn't need me but that I needed them."

I had known this woman for several years. I remembered her when she had happy, dancing eyes. I remembered the times when she could so easily throw her head back and laugh contagiously. But all the laughter and joy seemed to have died in her. I instinctively and compassionately embraced her, told her that we all make mistakes, and that the only important thing was to ask God's forgiveness and then to forgive herself. "We cannot sit forever in the darkness of regret. We can't make a career out of contrition." Her reply tore at my heart.

> But how can I forget? When I see a two-year-old, two years from now, you know what I will be thinking: "That's how old my baby would have been." And three years from now when I see a three-year-old . . . you know what I will be thinking. I finally did ask that nurse in the clinic for a glass of water and I ceremoniously poured it over my belly. I said softly, "Oh Baby, this is the best I can do for you. I baptize you in the Name of the Father . . . " If I ever get to heaven I hope I can see my baby there and tell him how sorry I am for what I have done.

My last vision of her face, as she was leaving me, stays with me—the sad eyes, the sad heart, the sad question: "How can I ever forget?"

The second woman was younger: a teenager, chewing bubblegum. She thought she was pregnant, but wasn't sure. When I asked her if the man with whom she had had intercourse knew of the possibility that she was carrying a child, her response somehow jolted me more deeply than the open agony of the first young woman: "Yeah, he knows. He said to get rid of the kid. He said it's like using a vacuum cleaner. He said he'd pay for half."

I spend a lot of my time at counseling. I watch people more closely than they know: their facial expressions, their vocal inflections, their body language. What disturbed me, during this interview, was that when this young girl said ". . . get rid of the kid," it didn't disturb her one bit. She did not look away, blink an eye, or miss a chew of her bubblegum. As she left me, I felt deep sadness, not only for her but for all the young people who have been victimized by the propaganda of the pro-abortionists. They have been brainwashed with the New Ethic which forbids any human being to be a burden or an inconvenience under pain of death. I thought to myself, as I saw the young girl disappear down the corridor, that the real casualty of all this propaganda is our humanity, our civilization. Is anyone there? Does anyone see what I see? Does anyone care?

The last of the three women was in her twenties. Her pregnancy had been confirmed by laboratory tests. She explained to me that she had stopped smoking and hadn't touched one drop of alcohol after the confirmation of her pregnancy. "Nicotine and alcohol," she reminded me, "can affect the baby." I was impressed with her unselfish concern for the other life inside her. Then she added, "But I have an appointment to kill this baby next Thursday morning." (I heard a soft "Oh my God!" inside me.)

61

I felt so sorry for that poor young woman. She was only one of a vast number of people whose lives, ideals, and morality are manipulated and dictated by the media. The media—the radio, television, and newspapers—warn us of the effects of nicotine and alcohol on a baby during the first nine months of its life. However, the same media also assure us that it is a valid (new) ethical and (newly) legalized choice to end that baby's life if we so choose. I had a sad feeling, as she was leaving, that my one voice was too weak to stand against the swelling chorus of voices, echoing the Supreme Court decision, which rationalized and legally inaugurated the New Ethic of utility and convenience. We reserve the right to kill you if you threaten to be a burden or an inconvenience.

Preparing for a Sabbatical

These three young women left me no choice. I could no longer turn away my head and be content to pay occasional lip service to the sanctity of human life. The questions I wanted to ask in Germany—Did you know? Did you do anything?—rose up to confront and haunt me. And so I asked for and was granted a sabbatical leave of absence from my university teaching post. In the several months preceding the sabbatical, I tried to research the situation and to find the place where I could best serve the cause of life and stem the tides of death.

Part of my research was to investigate the pro-abortion position. How would one argue for abortion? In the arenas of debate would I be told that abortion was not really the taking of an innocent human life? Those who had been active in the pro-life effort assured me that no one would argue for abortion in this way. The biological evidence is simply too compelling. The pro-life loyalists told me that their experience in direct dialogue with pro-abortionists was always the same. The argument always returns to the same refrain: "The abortion will save money, embarrassment, emotional stress. It will solve a problem of some kind." The pro-abortionists see themselves as heroes and humanists for tidying up some human ugliness. The fact that there is high cost in human life does not seem to concern them.

I still find it hard to believe that someone, balancing a human life against money and convenience on the scales of decision, could possibly choose the money and convenience and live with the destruction of human life. It is of course the blind selfishness of pragmatism and utilitarianism. Stripped of its propaganda euphemisms, it means simply that the end justifies the means even if the means involves the killing of an innocent human being.

Somehow I just can't take it in that America is really buying this thinly veiled Nazi doctrine: There are lives not worth living. Only those should be allowed to live who are wanted, who are productive, who are not physically handicapped or mentally retarded. Have American medical practitioners really volunteered, as some German doctors had once done, to become the social executioners of this neat little world that has no room for defectives? Just as I had trouble believing Sister Rutilia in the convent garden at Flittard until I read the confirmation of Dr. Alexander, so I couldn't believe what the pro-life proponents told me about the pro-abortion logic and strategy until I read confirmation in the statements of the pro-abortionists themselves.

The honest and outspoken among them have no difficulty admitting that an abortion is the taking of an innocent human life. The justification is indeed utility and convenience. William O. Douglas, the late Supreme Court justice, included in his opinion that a woman should be entitled to an abortion if having her baby "would alter her life style." I would like to list here some of the startling statements of pro-abortionists which I think are self-explanatory. The proponents of abortion, under all the euphemisms, are indeed aware of the terrible truth.

They Know What They Are Doing

In September, 1970, *Calfornia Medicine,* the voice of the California Medical Association, contained an editorial on the New Ethic. The editorial, entitled "A New Ethic for Medicine and Society," acknowledges that "since the old ethic [the reverence for life] has not yet been fully displaced [by the utilitarian principle], it has been necessary to separate the idea of abortion from the idea of killing."

The first task of the pro-abortion advocates was, therefore, the construction of a vocabulary of deception. It was a legal and societal necessity, a compromise of concealment. In the elaboration of such a vocabulary, the pro-abortionists even found a way to avoid mention of the human being (the baby) eliminated in an abortion. Any reference to

the victim would certainly raise questions, and the public was not yet sufficiently desensitized for this. The American people would have trouble with "killing a baby." So the favored phrase of the pro-abortion party came to be "the termination of a pregnancy." The editorial in *California Medicine* continued:

> The result has been a curious avoidance of the scientific fact, which everyone really knows, that human life begins at conception and is continuous whether intra- or extra-uterine until death. The very considerable semantic gymnastics which are required to rationalize abortion as anything but taking a human life would be ludicrous if they were not often put forth under socially impeccable auspices. [p. 68]

A strong pro-abortionist and propagandist, Dr. Mary Calderone, former medical director of Planned Parenthood, clearly admitted in an article in the *American Journal of Public Health* (vol. 50, no.7 [1960]):

> Abortion is the taking of a life. [p. 951]

Dr. Neville Sender, founder of the Metropolitan Medical Service, an abortion clinic in Milwaukee, Wisconsin, says:

> We know it is killing, but the states permit killing under certain circumstances.

Dr. Alan Guttmacher—late president of Planned Parenthood, even though his duties with Planned Parenthood have subsequently altered his perspectives—admitted in his book *Planning Your Family* (Macmillan, 1964) that the "exact moment" in the creation of a baby is fertilization.

Fertilization, then, has taken place; a baby has been conceived.

Dr. Bernard N. Nathanson is the former director of the Center for Reproductive and Sexual Health, the first and largest abortorium in the Western world. As we shall see later, Dr. Nathanson has reversed his position. His book *Aborting America* (Doubleday, 1979), coauthored by Richard N. Ostling, is one of the most significant books to be published since the Supreme Court decision. Dr. Nathanson remains a resolute atheist; he says that it was not religion but science that led him to change his mind about abortion. He writes:

> There is no longer any serious doubt in my mind that human life exists within the womb from the very onset of pregnancy.

Dr. Magda Denes, who has herself had an abortion, contends that abortions are both a necessity (because women need them) and a sorrow (because a human life is taken). Dr. Denes did two years of research in an abortorium and compiled the results of her research in a book, *In Necessity and Sorrow: Life and Death in an Abortion Hospital* (Basic Books, 1976). Later she told a Chicago newspaper:

> There wasn't a doctor who at one time or another in the questioning did not say, "This is murder." [*Daily News*, Oct. 22, 1976]

Dr. William Rashbaum, an abortionist who is chief of family planning services at Beth Israel Medical Center and a member of the faculty of the Albert Einstein College of Medicine, admitted in a newspaper interview that for a long time he was troubled in the midst of every abortion by the fantasy of the fetus hanging on to the walls of the uterus with tiny fingernails, resisting abortion with all its strength. He refers to the act of abortion as "destruction of life." In the *New York Times* magazine, April 17, 1977, he is quoted as saying:

> I'm a person. I'm entitled to my feelings. And my feelings are: Who gives me or anybody the right to terminate a pregnancy? I'm entitled to that feeling but I also have no right to communicate it to the patient. . . . I don't get paid for my feelings. I get paid for my skills.

The admission of these people who are professionally pro-abortion pioneers of the New Ethic is significant, I think. It is clear to them and to me that an abortion, however euphemistically it is described, is the taking of an innocent human life. The only alleged justification for this killing is convenience. It works. It solves a problem. It guarantees that defective or unwanted human beings will not prove a burden to the rest of us who are allowed to live. It is the New Ethic.

Congressional Hearings

On April 23 and 24, 1981, the U.S. Congress took the historic step of holding hearings on "the question of when human life begins." In its decision legalizing abortion-on-demand, the Supreme Court asserted that it could not resolve "the difficult question of when human life begins," and so the Court proceeded to legalize abortion throughout the full nine months of pregnancy. One medical school professor, Dr. Eugene Diamond, has said that "either the justices were fed a backwoods biology or they were pretending ignorance about a scientific certainty" (personal communication). For myself, I cannot believe that the learned justices did not know the scientific facts. As the editorial on the New Ethic in *California Medicine* said very clearly, in 1970: There is "a curious avoidance of the scientific fact, which everyone really knows, that human life begins at conception."

At any rate, a group of internationally known geneticists appeared before a Senate judiciary subcommittee to tell Congress that human life "begins at the moment of conception." Senator Max Baucus (D. Montana), a pro-abortionist member of the separation of powers subcommittee, had been invited by the staff to submit a list of pro-abortion witnesses who would testify that life begins at some time other than fertilization. Senator Baucus failed to produce any such witnesses in the first round of hearings. Professor Leon Rosenberg, the lone pro-abortion witness at the hearings, did not address the question of when life begins, but simply dismissed the question as a religious and metaphysical issue. He insisted that the question of when life begins is not a scientific question. Rosenberg anticipated the almost unbelievable resolution of the National Academy of Sciences, made shortly after the Senate hearings, that the question of the beginning of life must be answered by theologians, not by scientists. (Galileo must have turned over in his grave!)

What grounds will the pro-abortionists stand on if not on scientific grounds? They have been maintaining for years that religious arguments are not relevant to public policy. The moment of fertilization itself is an almost miraculous explosion, with billions of complex designs being made very rapidly, with bits of information unfolding at incredible speeds. The creative, organizing force is obviously not the mother or the father. Most of us call this creative force God, others call it nature, and some attribute it to the child itself. This magnificent miracle of creative power should inspire wonder and awe. The only logical abortionist position is rejection of such considerations. It is obvious to me that public opinion and policy should be based on scientifically verifiable facts. Here are excerpts from the testimony of the world's leading geneticists before the Senate subcommittee on separation of powers.

Dr. Jerome LeJeune, professor of fundamental genetics at the University of Descarte, Paris, France:

> When does a person begin? I will try to give the most precise answer to that question actually available to science. Modern biology teaches us that ancestors are united to their progeny by a continuous material link, for it is from the fertilization of the female cell (the ovum) by the male cell (the spermatozoa) that a new member of the species will emerge. Life has a very, very long history but each individual has a very neat beginning, *the moment of its conception*. . . . To accept that fact that after fertilization has taken place, a new human has come into being, is no longer a matter of taste or of opinion. The human nature of the human being from conception to old age is not a metaphysical contention, it is plain experimental evidence. [italics added]

Dr. Micheline Matthews-Roth, principal research associate of the Harvard University Medical School:

In biology and in medicine, it is an accepted fact that the life of any individual organism reproducing by sexual reproduction begins at conception (fertilization), the time when the egg cell from the female and the sperm cell from the male join to form a single new cell, the zygote; this zygote is the starting cell of the new organism. . . . [Dr. Matthews-Roth proceeded to quote from eight biology textbooks which stated that life begins at conception.] You will notice that I have been using the words fertilization and conception interchangeably. It is very important that in drafting the statute the word "conception" be specifically defined as meaning the time of the fusion of the egg cell and the sperm cell. This is important because there seems to be a tendency in some medical circles to define conception as being the time of the implantation of the developing embryo in the wall of the uterus rather than the time of fertilization of the egg by the sperm. It is crucial to remember, since implantation occurs about 6 to 10 days after fertilization, that the zygote is already well on its way in the process of development by the time implantation occurs. . . . In summary, then, it is incorrect to say that biological data cannot be decisive. . . . So, therefore, *it is scientifically correct to say that an individual human life begins at conception,* when the egg and sperm join to form the zygote, and that this developing human always is a member of our species in all stages of its life. Our laws, one function of which is to help preserve the lives of our people, should be based on accurate scientific data. [italics added]

Professor Hymie Gordon, chairman of the Department of Medical Genetics at the Mayo Clinic:

Thus, from the moment of conception the organism contains many complex molecules; it synthesizes new intricate structures from simple raw materials; and it replicates itself. *By all the criteria of modern molecular biology, life is present from the moment of conception.* [italics added]

71

Dr. McCarthy DeMere, lawyer and practicing physician, and law professor at the University of Tennessee:

> From the medical standpoint there are mountains of documents to show that the human embryo is a separate person, biologically distinct from the mother. . . . From both the legal and medical standpoint, there is absolutely no question in my mind and I feel in the minds of most individuals who have given serious thought to this question, *the exact moment of the beginning [of] personhood and of the human body is at the moment of conception.* [italics added]

Dr. Alfred Bongiovanni, formerly chairman of pediatrics at the University of Ife in Nigeria and currently a member of the University of Pennsylvania Medical School faculty:

> I have learned since my earliest medical education that *human life begins at the time of conception.* The standard textbooks which were used in the courses I took, many of them in continuous use until today, so state it. . . . I am no more prepared to say that these early stages represent an incomplete human being than I would be to say that the child prior to the dramatic events of puberty which I have outlined is not a human being. This is human life at every stage albeit incomplete until late adolescence. [italics added]

Dr. Jasper Williams, of the Williams Clinic in Chicago, and past president of the National Medical Association:

> Human life's singular characteristic is mental behavior associated with development of genetically influenced bodily characteristics. . . . This process begins when the sperm fertilizes the ovum. . . . The work of Edwards and his associates in England with test tube babies has repeatedly proved that *human life begins*

when after the ovum is fertilized the new combined cell mass begins to divide. [italics added]

Dr. Watson A. Bowes, Jr., of the University of Colorado Medical School:

> But one thing is clear. Following fertilization there is an inexorable series of events that unfolds with cells dividing, moving, pausing, differentiating, and aggregating with a baffling precision and purpose. In the early hours, days, and weeks of this development a hypothetical observer, if able to witness this microscopic drama, would find it impossible to identify precisely when major qualitative changes have occurred just as parents observing daily their child's growth and development cannot say precisely when he or she stopped being a child and became an adult. . . . Thus the beginning of a single human life is from a biological point of view a simple and straightforward matter—*the beginning is conception.* . . . In conclusion, *the beginning of a human life from a biological point of view is at the time of conception.* This straightforward biological fact should not be distorted to serve sociological, political, or economic goals. [italics added]

These are the testimonies of some of the world's leading geneticists. Their testimony before Congress was unanimous. Dr. Harold W. Manner, chairman of the Department of Biology at Loyola University of Chicago, adds: "When a human sperm fertilizes a human egg, the result is a human being—from the moment of conception. The killing of this living human being must be considered homicide." (personal communication)

CHAPTER 6

HOW DID WE GET THERE?
The Architects
and Their Plans

"We fed the public a line of deceit, dishonesty, a fabrication of statistics and figures. We succeeded [in breaking down the laws limiting abortions] because the time was right and the news media cooperated. We sensationalized the effects of illegal abortions, and fabricated polls which indicated that 85 percent of the public favored unrestricted abortion, when we knew it was only 5 percent. We unashamedly lied, and yet our statements were quoted [by the media] as though they had been written in law."

—Dr. Bernard N. Nathanson,
from an address to the
Winnipeg League for Life,
April 25, 1981

How Did We Get There?

If all this be true, the question obviously arises: How did we get there? How have we become so insensitive to the value of each and every human life? How were we deceived by the propaganda? Why have so many American doctors caved in? How could the justices of the Supreme Court legalize the killing of babies during all nine months of pregnancy? How do we turn away our eyes from the American "killing centers"?

This part of the manuscript for this book was written on the Memorial Day weekend—a time when the newscasters keep us painfully aware of highway fatalities. A friend of mine just an hour ago remarked to me that there have been 149 traffic fatalities already on this weekend, which is only half over. He underlined his own personal sadness and horror: "Those 149 lives were human lives. They were people. It wasn't just pieces of steel colliding with pieces of steel. Human lives were lost!"

I conceded that the highway carnage was deeply saddening. Then I remarked, "However, what bothers me much more is the four thousand babies that die each day in this country by abortions. They do not die by accident. They are deliberately killed. They are real human beings. It's not just suction machines or saline injections salting out growths or curettes cutting away a piece of something. They are real people, real human beings. Four thousand every day." My friend looked at me, rather puzzled. "That's right, isn't it?" he said almost absently as he turned to walk away.

Persons/Things

I personally suspect that our problems began with a heavily commercialized approach to the "good life." The script reads that we should go through life with the maximum amount of pleasure and the minimum amount of pain. "Eat this delicious food." "Sleep on this form-fitting mattress." "Pop this pill." "Fly now, pay later!" We must shun suffering of all kinds. Suffering has nothing to say to us. And we must anesthetize immediately all pain. Deluged by this presentation of the good life, we have experienced a societal confusion between living a good life and having a good time. Living a good life almost always exacts some price and asks for some commitment. Such a challenge is alien to those committed to "having a good time."

The biblical formula for a good life is this: "Love persons/Use things." When God made the world he saw that it was very good. The world is charged, indeed, with the grandeur of God. And he calls upon us to join him in that pronouncement: "It is very good!" We are invited to use and to enjoy all God's good things. But we are warned: Don't ever let your heart be owned by things. If you *love* things, you will soon begin *using* persons to get, or get more of, the things you love. Save your heart for love, and save your love for persons.

The biblical imperative is illustrated by an example from the life of Martin Buber, the "I-Thou" philosopher. Buber directed his philosophical speculation toward "I-Thou" matters, toward the primacy of persons, after a very sad incident. A young man came to Buber's office one day, asking

77

for some time. "I need to see you." Buber declined on the grounds that he was preparing a paper for delivery at a convention at a later date. That night the young man killed himself. His suicide touched Buber very deeply. In a renewed and painful way, he learned the importance of loving persons and using things.

This "Love persons/Use things" is a delicate equilibrium that is easily unbalanced. The moment that we start loving things we begin to use people to get the things we love. Consequently, the Bible does not say that "money is the root of all evil." It says that "*love of* money is the root of all evil." Where your treasure is there your heart will be. When we get hooked, for example, on praise and adulation, we allow entrance into our world only to those who bring with them the necessary price of admission. When we get hooked on our own pleasures and satisfactions, we refuse to allow a place in our world for those who might be a burden or an inconvenience. We will not accept the challenge of love.

I think that we have been thoroughly drenched with the message of our own enjoyment. We have been seduced by the propaganda of personal pleasure. We have quarantined out of sight anything that threatens to deprive us of our personal satisfactions. We are pleasure seekers and power brokers. Butterflies are free. A spate of literature has helped us to rationalize this manipulation of others, this preference of things to people. We have successfully inverted the biblical principle. We now can unashamedly love things and use people. There are still audible a few dying gasps of our societal conscience. We hear protests against too much sex and excessive violence, but the purveyors of sex and violence reassure us that they sell. This is what people want. "Whatever sells, whatever works . . . is good."

Secular Humanism

Denial of traditional religious values has certainly given further momentum to the death-on-demand movement. Former Congressman John Conlan of Arizona has remarked:

> There is a significant trend in education today to teach children that there are no values, that there is no right, that there is no wrong, that there is no God, that man is his own God.

This would certainly be the suggestion of American secular humanism, which has taken such a strong hold on the modern American mentality. It is perhaps the strongest philosophical force pushing us along the course of the abortion-euthanasia, death-on-demand mentality.

The secular humanist creed was first codified in 1933 when American humanists, under the leadership of John Dewey, philosopher and educator, drew up the "Humanist Manifesto." Dewey, a humanist and pragmatist, has had an enormous effect on American education.

The manifesto bristles with hostility against traditional religion. It boldly declares that there is no God and that religious belief is an obstacle to human progress. Only rationality and science can save us.

In 1973 the manifesto was updated. Its major themes were repeated in a humanist declaration,

published in the September/October, 1980, issue of *The Humanist*. It reads in part:

> We believe, however, that traditional dogmatic or authoritarian religions that place revelation, God, ritual, or creed above human needs and experience do a disservice to the human species. Any account of nature should pass the tests of scientific evidence; in our judgment, the dogmas and myths of traditional religions do not do so. . . . We find insufficient evidence for belief in the existence of a supernatural; it is either meaningless or irrelevant to the question of the survival and fulfillment of the human race. . . .
>
> No deity will save us; we must save ourselves. . . .
>
> We strive for the good life, here and now. [pp. 6, 7]

Traditional religions enjoin us to love one another as brothers and sisters of the same common father, God: "Whatever you do to the least of my children . . ." Traditional religions forbid us to kill one another: "Thou shalt not kill!" Obviously such religions must be declared "meaningless and irrelevant." All the emphasis must be put on "the good life here and now." I must get the biggest cut of the cake I can. Love . . . brother/sisterhood . . . the human family of God—such ideas "do a disservice to the human species." Sidney Simon, author of "values clarification" books which are widely used in schools, insists that "we don't need any more preaching about right and wrong . . . the old 'thou shalt nots' simply are not relevant."

Societal Rationalization

Societal rationalization of evil is a group process, a perversion of public decency and morals by mutual cooperation. "Everybody's doing it. Look at the movies. Look at TV. Art imitates life. That's

81

the way it is." In the great tides of such public opinion and propaganda, the average person just floats along. He or she doesn't have to do all the work of rationalizing, making wrong seem and sound as if it were right. This is already done by society. "Everybody's doing it." If you're not doing it, you're not "with it."

An essential part of this process of societal rationalization is cleaning up the language. Language is something like the sugar coating of the ideas which we swallow and digest. And ideas have serious consequences. It's a lot easier to swallow dishonesty if you call it "a fast buck" or "easy money." It's a lot easier to commit adultery if you trivialize it as "fooling around." Fornication is "swinging." It's a lot easier to kill a baby if you call it "terminating a pregnancy." It's a lot easier to discuss abortion if you never mention the tiny human victim or refer to the victim's death.

Reenter Doctor Nathanson

Dr. Bernard Nathanson is a key figure in the whole American abortion tragedy. It was he, with others, who organized the repeal of abortion laws. It was he who supervised the largest and busiest abortion mill in the world, the Center for Reproductive and Sexual Health in New York City. In the first year of his tenure the Center had performed more than sixty thousand abortions. At this point Dr. Nathanson admitted to being "deeply troubled by my own increasing certainty that I had in fact presided over sixty thousand deaths." To his great credit, he acted on his new insights and completely reversed his position.

Remaining a "resolute atheist," Dr. Nathanson was convinced by science, by the expanding knowledge of conception (fertilization) and fetal life, that "a human life is at stake." He says that "biology requires any civilized society to react with revulsion at the Supreme Court's policy of abortion on request for any reason; when the embryo or fetus is there—alive—an inescapable part of the human community." (*Chicago Sun-Times*, Dec. 11, 1979)

As to Dr. Nathanson's part in and explanation of the rationalization and legalization of abortion, it would be better, I think, to let him tell his own story. The remarks quoted here are from an address given at the National Right to Life Convention, 1980:

> I want to take you back some twelve years to 1968 at which time I, and later Betty Friedan and Carol Grietzer, organized a political action group known as the National Association for Repeal of Abortion Laws. We organized it as a tight, well-structured, and dynamic little cadre. It was the right time. Feminism was on the move, the Vietnam War was raging, authority was being destroyed everywhere and, very important to all of us here, there was no organization of those opposed to abortion.

> There was only silence from the opposition. We fed a line of deceit, of dishonesty, of fabrication of statistics and figures; we coddled, caressed, and stroked the press. We cadged money from various sources and we, in one short year, succeeded in striking down the abortion laws of New York State and in one fell swoop established the city of New York as the abortion capital of the world. We were calling ourselves pro-abortionists and pro-choice. In fact what we were were abortifiers: those who like abortion.

Let me digress and speak for a moment on the question of "pro-choice," as they euphemistically call themselves now. I reject that phrase, that euphemism. It is misleading. It is dishonest. It implies that in the issue of abortion there is an ethical choice whether to have an abortion or whether not to have an abortion; and how can you be against choice? Of course, the joker in that deck is that abortion is not an ethical choice, and therefore that is not an ethical choice at all, and therefore there is no such thing as pro-choice in abortions. With the striking down of the New York law, and following it, three years later, the Supreme Court's infamous decision, we had effected a social revolution, the consequences of which have polluted this nation perhaps more profoundly than any single political act of its time in America. That act, permissive abortion, was and is a singular specimen of that special brand of twentieth-century madness.

In February of 1971, having completed the housekeeping details on breaking the law in New York State, I organized and ran the Center for Reproductive and Sexual Health, another amusing euphemism for an abortion clinic. It was not just an abortion clinic. It was *the* abortion clinic. It was in New York City and curiously, Ladies and Gentlemen, it was established and fed by the Clergy Consultation Service, an organization of twelve hundred Protestant ministers and Jewish rabbis who took it upon themselves to funnel through sixty thousand young women in the space of the nineteen months that I ran it. The Clergy Consultation Service—I'd never known that clergymen were actively involved in abortion before, but my eyes were really opened. The clinic functioned on a twelve-hour, sometimes a sixteen-hour day: 8 A.M. to midnight, 120 abortions a day, Sundays included. It was a $5-million-a-year business, a $5-million-a-year business! Think, think now how many handicapped children could be helped, how much cancer research could be done, how many operations of a decent sort could be carried out on poor people with that kind of money!

I was up to my knees and elbows in blood in that place. When I took it over, there was a staff of thirty-five physicians who were really an incredible band of ruffians, bandits, rogues, and literally fugitives from the FBI. . . . I stayed there and ran that operation for nineteen months. In the words of Yeats, the great Irish poet, "The blood-dimmed tide is loosed and everywhere a ceremony of innocence was drowned."

. . . Why did I change my mind? Well, to begin with, it was not from religious conviction, because as I have stated on many occasions in front of many of you, as I have stated in this book [*Aborting America*] which is public record, I am an atheist, quite frankly. . . . In any case, the change of mind began with the realization, the inescapable reality that the fetus, that embryo, is a person, is a protectable human life. The change also began on the basis of my own secular belief in the golden rule: If you would not have your own life taken away from you, you must not take someone else's life.

The discussion . . . has been muddied by a resort to a particularly vicious brand of anti-Catholicism, as many of you know, in the press. There have been ongoing attempts to paint this movement [the Pro-Life movement] as a Catholic movement, and there have been almost heartbreaking lies and libel in the press on this score. If you ever substituted for the word *Catholic*, in many of these publications, the word *Jewish* or *black*, you would be immediately castigated. The press would destroy you. However, because the word *Catholic* is used, it appears to be allowable.

My opinion, my feeling, is this regarding the anti-Catholic issue and the religious issue: the anti-abortion conviction is no more a religious position than the civil rights issue was. . . . Let me remind you that the civil rights movement in this country was led by a Protestant clergyman, the Rev. Martin Luther King, and it was preached from a great many pulpits across this land. Yet I cannot recall the press or the media in those years denigrating or dismissing the civil rights movement as merely a religious issue or accusing those who supported the movement of violating the first amendment rights of others, as the Honorable Judge Dooling has done in Brooklyn in the McRae case.

[Here Dr. Nathanson quotes from his editorial published in 1974 in the *New England Journal of Medicine*, entitled "Deeper into Abortion." In it Dr. Nathanson reflected his change of mind and troubled conscience.] ". . . I am deeply troubled by my own increasing certainty that I had, in fact, presided over sixty thousand deaths. There is no longer serious doubt in my mind that human life exists within the womb, from the very onset of pregnancy. . . . To those who cry that nothing can be human life that cannot exist independently, I ask: Is the patient totally dependent for his life on treatments by the artificial kidney twice weekly, is he alive? Is the person with chronic cardiac disease solely dependent for his life on the tiny batteries in his pacemaker—alive? Would my life be safe in this city without my eyeglasses? Life is an interdependent phenomenon for us all. It is a continuous spectrum that begins in the uterus and that ends at death. . . . Abortion must be seen as the interruption of a process which would otherwise have produced a citizen of the world. Denial of this reality is the crassest kind of moral evasiveness."

[Dr. Nathanson comments here about the reaction to that editorial piece.] . . . The vicious letters, the telephone calls, the threats that I received were simply innumerable and obscene. Of course, we were socially outcast from our friends, our previous friends in the abortifier movement. In fact, I was summoned to a kangaroo court of the Committee of the National Association for Repeal of Abortion Laws to explain and justify what I had done and, of course, declined gracefully the invitation.

Francis Bacon once said, "If a man will begin with certainties, he shall end in doubts. But if he will be content to begin with doubts, he will end with certainties." I think this really sums up my intellectual odyssey on this question.

So now I am joined with you [Pro-Life people] irrevocably in this cause. That we have endured a succession of setbacks is undeniable. But we must not flag or fail. Each one us, even the smallest and the most insignificant, is essential to the continued struggle for this cause. Remember one person with courage is a majority. This fight must go on to eradicate the evil of abortion in this land. As Abraham Lincoln once said, "No policy that does not rest on decent public opinion can be permanently maintained."

What is our task? To make this country a place for decent people to live in! What is our end? To call an immediate halt to the senseless destruction of our greatest natural resource, our children! In closing, let me leave you with this admonition, again spoken in the words of the great Edmund Burke, but still as relevant and as important as it was two hundred years ago, "The only thing necessary for the triumph of evil is for good men to do nothing."

Aborting America

Dr. Nathanson and Richard Ostling's book, *Aborting America*, is a startling exposé of the pro-abortion movement. Nathanson has charged the pro-abortion forces with a "systematic suppression of this book." He claims that all word about this book has been "totally blacked out" in New York City. The *New York Times* has on five occasions refused to review it.

In the book, Dr. Nathanson admits that he was "a utilitarian in my ethic until 1973 or 1974." He now believes that "an unexamined utilitarian ethos and a corresponding 'situation ethic' have led to this monstrous abortion situation." He clearly repudiates such utilitarianism as a viable moral code for a civilized society.

> Instead of cherishing the individual human life, we are calculating the "greatest good for the greatest number," which translates into "quality of life," "cost/benefit," an "improved human race." . . . As Professor Rawls protests so elegantly, a decision that increases the general happiness may be unjust. For instance, it may be made at the expense of a minority group. I would add that of such groups, the intra-uterine population is the most defenseless of all. I can no longer subscribe to this dehumanizing ethic. [p. 251]

Later, citing the editorial on the New Ethic in *California Medicine* (which we have mentioned extensively), Nathanson writes:

> If abortion is not justified as a "right," then it must be justified on pragmatic grounds, very often variations on the "unwanted child" theme. This deserves the most careful consideration for, as *California Medicine* sensed, it is a seismic shift in the philosophy of our civilization. The value of life is subjective. Life or death is a matter of whether "I" want "you" or whether "we" want "them" to live. Life in and of itself is no longer treated as having intrinsic worth. This wholesale retreat from the Hippocratic code should be and has been particularly difficult for physicians to stomach. [p. 253]

It should be recalled that in the editorial in *California Medicine*, the obvious logical connection between birth selection and death selection was pointed out. Speaking of the part doctors play in making life-or-death decisions, it said: "One may anticipate further development of these roles as the problems of birth control and birth selection are extended inevitably to death selection and death control whether by the individual or by society" (p. 68).

Nathanson also speaks of the "conflict between the Old Morality and the New Morality." He points out that, in its abortion decisions, "the Supreme Court relied on the 'right of privacy,' following reasoning that stands up only if alpha [Nathanson's designation of the fetus] is demonstrably not human life. To say that it is *not* human life is a statement of faith, one that flies in the face of biology."

The most surprising revelation in *Aborting America* was for me the revelation of a decision made by the pro-abortionists in the beginning. They decided that the New Ethic and New Morality, which could handle the rationalization of abortion and promote its legislation, could be force-fed to the American public if abortion were presented as a "Catholic issue" and a "feminist issue." The architect of this strategy was, according to Nathanson, one Lawrence Lader, a virulent anti-Catholic bigot. Nathanson writes of the first suggestion of this strategy by Lader:

> "Historically," he [Lader] said after the usual throat-clearing ceremony, "every revolution has to have its villain. It doesn't really matter whether it's a king, a dictator, or a tsar, but it has to be *someone,* a person, to rebel against. It's easier for the people we want to persuade to perceive it in this way." I conceded that. It was good tactical strategy. . . . [Lader continued,] "A single person isn't quite what we want, since that might excite sympathy for him. Rather, a small group of shadowy, powerful people. *Too* large a group would diffuse the focus, don't you see? . . . You know who I mean, Bernie."

Not the Catholics again? . . . It was his devil theory.

"Not just all Catholics. First of all, that's too large a group, and for us to vilify them all would diffuse our focus. Secondly, we have to convince liberal Catholics to join us, a popular front as it were, and if we tar them all with the same brush, we'll just antagonize a few who might otherwise have joined us and be valuable showpieces for us. No, it's got to be the Catholic *hierarchy*. That's a small enough group to cone [sic] down on, and anonymous enough so that no names ever have to be mentioned, but everybody will have a fairly good idea whom we are talking about."

. . . "We've got to keep the women out in front," he [Lader] asserted. "You know what I mean." Yes, I did. And that made eminent political sense, too. "And some blacks. Black women especially. Why are they so damned slow to see the importance of this whole movement to themselves?" . . . "All we've got is Mrs. Fisher, who is somewhere to the right of Marie Antoinette," he gloomed. [pp. 51-53]

In the light of this revelation, it is interesting to look back over some of the things written in the NARAL (National Abortion Rights Action League, formerly called the National Association for Repeal of Abortion Laws) appeals and general correspondence. One of their appeals reads as follows: "Please help us to turn Congress around by informing American voters of the shameful capitulation to vocal religious minorities that resulted in the Medicaid Abortion ban." From the correspondence of the same organization, we read: "The American voters need to know the full story of the abortion issue. They need to know that Congress has capitulated to the pressure of lobbying that is largely supported by the hierarchy of the Catholic Church."

Finally, it is interesting to notice that the proposed strategy was accepted and implemented by Planned Parenthood, one of the two most powerful propagandists for abortion-on-demand. Two years ago Planned Parenthood hired a black woman, Faye Wattleton, at seventy thousand dollars a year, to become its president. She is anything but to the right of Marie Antoinette. In one of her initial statements, made in the May 22, 1978, issue of *People Magazine,* she said: "We've allowed Right-to-Lifers to have center stage. . . . But those days are over."

The Human Life Center, in Collegeville, Minnesota, published a flyer listing the following facts about the Planned Parenthood Federation: "In 1975 about 35,000 abortions were performed at Planned Parenthood abortoriums. The number of their referrals to other abortion centers is not known. According to Planned Parenthood's Five Year Plan they [had hoped] to perform 80,000 abortions a year by 1980." All this is interesting in the light of the fact that in 1963 a pamphlet that was put out by Planned Parenthood stated: "An abortion kills the life of a baby after it has begun. It is dangerous to your life and health. It may make you sterile so that when you want a child you cannot have it." That was written, of course, before the New Ethic came to Planned Parenthood under the leadership of Dr. Alan Guttmacher.

Planned Parenthood's youth activities and so-called "sex education" amount to a positive encouragement of sexual activity among teenagers. Their provocative literature results in a tremendous peer pressure that makes teenagers who do not engage in sex feel abnormal. Some of their literature has even suggested that a young person might have to choose between having sex and being lonely. Planned Parenthood is certainly creating a demand for its own services.

On the so-called "Catholic issue," Dr. Harold O. J. Brown, chairman of the Christian Action Council and a leading Protestant theologian, wrote in a letter to "Fellow Christians" on December 1, 1975:

> Although there is almost no other moral issue on which Christian witness has been so united through the ages, pro-abortion activists never miss an opportunity to stamp abortion a "Catholic issue." They realize that if they can make abortion look like the specific concern of a particular minority, they can in effect silence the tens of millions of other Americans—the majority, I have no doubt—who also feel strongly about abortion. . . . What this means, in effect, is that our laws will be influenced only by that small minority who repudiate our whole Christian heritage and everything that it has meant to our civilization and society. . . . I know that, while there are differences with respect to details of application, almost all Christians here and abroad share our concern about abortion, and recognize the horror of our present abortion-on-demand situation.

CHAPTER 7

THE SABBATICAL EXPERIENCE
"It's the Law of the Land!"

"Historians say that Justice Taney thought that his decision in Dred Scott would lay to rest the issue of slavery. Whether the seven Justices are so sanguine or deceived as to think that they have resolved the issue of abortion cannot be known. What they may have done in effect is to stimulate a renewed and fortified popular struggle for the rights of all human beings, the unborn as well as those who have proved their viability."

—J. Robert Nelson,
professor of theology at
Boston University, from
"Confusion at the Highest Level"
in *The Christian Century*
(Feb. 28, 1973, p.254)

The Sabbatical Experience

In the two years following the Supreme Court decision my own shock and sadness became increasingly painful. Eventually silence became unbearable. As mentioned earlier, I took a sabbatical leave of absence from teaching and spent the whole of 1976 as a spokesman for the pro-life cause. At the beginning of this year, a close friend, who had been locked into the pro-life struggle for years, wrote to me: "John, prepare yourself. You have been used to success, to applause, to melting hearts and winning people over. This year, on the pro-life circuit, will be very different and very difficult for you. This will be your 'desert' year." Thus forewarned, with the fearful reluctance of Jeremiah, with the zealous eagerness of Isaiah, I set out into the desert.

The first thing I noticed was my suddenly diminished popularity as a speaker. Ordinarily I get three to five requests a day for speaking engagements. (I didn't know how to say that modestly, so I just said it.) I have to choose among these invitations selectively. During 1976 I would agree to speak anywhere, at any time, and without any fee. Only one stipulation: I would speak only on the right of every human being to life. When I made this known to those inviting me to speak to their groups, the usual response was, "Oh, that's too bad. We had wanted you to speak on some other topic, any other topic." One large religious group asked me to keynote their annual convention on any subject of my choice. I agreed, but informed the caller that my subject would be "The Right to Life." He immediately withdrew the invitation. He said somewhat apologetically, "I'm truly sorry, but you might upset the delegates at the convention if you speak on that topic." I accepted his decision, but told him that this was an essential part of my vocation: to comfort the afflicted and to afflict the comfortable.

Over the course of the year, however, I did manage several invitations a week with groups that agreed to accept me as a pro-life spokesperson. Many of these invitations involved a respondent, who would "give the other side." Some were openly called "debates." If the year wasn't a desert, it was surely hot out there: truly a purification. Several times groups engaged me to speak without including the subject of my speech in promotional materials. The result was definitely "an experience." When I announced my subject, a very few were happy. Another and larger group paraphrased, "Thanks! I needed that." A vocal minority, perhaps ten to twenty percent, felt misled and voiced their regret. And there were always a few who walked out on me. It is an intact record that I have never once spoken on the right to life without someone leaving. Twice I was interrupted by shouts. Nevertheless there was an enormous consolation in all this. My encounters with people during this year proved again to me that most people are basically decent. Most of the people I encountered seemed open to the message of the sacredness of human life.

Still I felt something like the center on a football team. I knew that as soon as I snapped the ball (talked on the right to life and against abortion), there would be a painful impact of collision. By the year's end I was getting used to this. The

bruises never lasted very long, and I have always maintained that all of us need some purification of our motives by adversity. (At least that's what I say.)

The Arguments . . . The Ignorance . . . The Agonies

Even though I was warned to anticipate them, the biggest surprise of my sabbatical year was the arguments of those who doubted and questioned me. In one way or another, most of the questions seemed to be a rerun of Hegelian utilitarianism. The old pan scales, the baby weighed against money, embarrassment, inconvenience, and so forth. And the language was always the same: "termination of pregnancy" without mention of the victim. The reasoning usually prescinded from morality, focusing rather on practicality and the *quality-of-life* ethic. Make the world better and life easier for us. The "good life here and now"— for us! The end justifies the means.

One woman from the Planned Parenthood Federation promised that she would be on my side if I could find a way to solve all the problems that she was solving so quickly and easily by a two-hundred-dollar abortion. One minister of religion reassured our audience that he would judge no one. Especially would he lay no "guilt trips" on anyone. He accused me of doing just this by insisting that abortion is the act of taking an innocent human life. (I later sent him a gift copy of Dr. Menninger's book *Whatever Became of Sin?* [Hawthorn, 1973], the famous psychiatrist's complaint that the clergy today is unwilling to condemn evil.)

One political science professor at a university

suggested, in debate, that if a woman were practicing birth control and discovered herself to be pregnant, it would be analogous to locking the doors of her house and coming home to find that an unwelcome intruder had invaded her home. "She has the right to kill that intruder. She has the right to kill the baby because it, too, is an unwelcome intruder." This statement actually drew a smattering of applause.

My own pro-life presentation was given without slides or vivid pictures. In general it followed the same "personal progression" of this book. At one college a young woman-student began to weep uncontrollably during my presentation. Later she said that she had gone to Planned Parenthood because "they promised counseling." Once there, she reported, the counseling consisted in a discussion of "when I wanted it [the abortion] done." As she was listening to me speaking about the fetus as an independent human life, she admitted, "It was the first time I ever realized that I was making a moral choice, a choice of life or death . . . and I had made the wrong choice!"

The Clergy and Guilt

Another insight of the "desert year" was the reluctance of the clergy to preach or speak about abortion. During the sabbatical year I spoke to a relatively large group (thirty to fifty) of clergy once a week. I tried to outline for them an effective presentation of the pro-life argumentation. They were, like most audiences, interested and polite. At the end of my presentation, however, I was customarily surrounded by a small group inviting me "to come to my church and give this talk." I sensed that their reluctance grew out of a fear that an open condemnation of abortion might alienate them from part of their congregation. Such a condemnation might upset those women in the church who had already had abortions and those men who had been a party to abortions.

I myself have been very sensitive to this latter concern. In my own preaching and teaching, I have tried to remain on the level of objective morality without judging the personal, subjective responsibility of those who might have had or been a partner to an abortion. For me there is an obvious and clear distinction between judging an action and judging the moral responsibility of a person. It is a critically important distinction to make clear when one is speaking about abortion.

If a person takes the life of an innocent human being, this action is in itself disordered. However, the person who took the life might have been insane (at least temporarily), might not have realized what he/she was doing (like the young college woman), might have taken the life by accident of miscalculation. These are the things that the jury in a courtroom must try to decide during legal trials. Clearly I am a jury to the conscience of no other man or woman. However, sane or insane, realizing or not realizing, by accident or on purpose, the act of taking the life of an innocent human being was, is, and always will be a disordered action. The person perpetrating the deed may have been subjectively innocent by reason of insanity, ignorance, or miscalculation.

It is, of course, possible to speak about the biological facts, to quote even the most zealous pro-abortion doctors to the effect that the fetus really is a human being, undeniably possessing human life. The killing of such a fetus is, like it or not, the killing of a human person, a homicide. It is possible to speak about the monstrous and dehumanizing effects of legalizing this killing, and even to present the religious dimensions of this killing, without in any way passing judgment on the personal guilt of any of those in the audience. I remember one night a young woman, in a church-related group, coming up to me at the end of my presentation. She hugged me gratefully and whispered in my ear:

> Thanks for what you said. Four years ago I had an abortion. I tried to look away, to forget what I had done. But it kept haunting me, like the skeleton in the closet. Tonight while you were talking I gave up my pretense of looking away. I faced it. I asked God to forgive me and to take care of the baby. Then I forgave myself. Tonight, for the first time since the abortion, I feel peace, deep peace, about the whole thing.

It is difficult to speak about evil, especially about the evil of abortion. If the societal rationalization is unraveled, if the euphemisms are lifted, and if all the facts are clearly exposed, some people will have to deal with guilt and remorse. The same thing is true, no matter what the evil. One can only hope that those who have to deal with personal guilt will deal with it constructively and not make a lifetime career out of remorse. There is no punishment worse than living forever in the darkened room of self-condemnation. In general, a person is much better off in taking and facing full responsibility for his/her life and actions than in trying to live a lie or play out a charade. The skeleton always rattles in the closet. The wood held under water is always trying to rise to the surface. Denial of our guilt is always exhausting. Confession is indeed good for the soul.

While speaking of the clergy, I must admit something else. One of the sharpest edges of my own personal disappointment came out of the knowledge that many of the clergy of various denominations were in fact pro-abortion. One minister was even president of the National Abortion Rights Action League. He was always attacking pro-life groups. His argument: "A legal abortion for a woman on welfare now costs the state $150, but if the abortion were not performed the state would pay out $60,000 over an 18-year span to support the mother and child on welfare." The old pan scales. The choice, he suggests, should be obvious.

I have never understood how a minister of the Gospel could assure his congregation of God's love, and somehow not extend that love of God to the preborn. It seems to me that it would demand some kind of a split in the personality to say to a congregation, "The good news is that God loves you!" and to say to the four thousand unborn who perish each day in our country, ". . . but not you. You see, you are not wanted." How does such a minister of the good news come face to face in prayer with the Lord who said, "Whatever you do to the least of my children . . ."?

"The Law of the Land"

Of course, in public discussions which lead to

the formation of public policy, religious motivation and the enlightenment of God's Word are not acceptable or appropriate. Separation of Church and State. "No Bible quoting, please." I understand and accept this. However, it really pains me to hear people quoting the gospel according to Justice Blackmun and the Supreme Court. "It's the [infallible] Law of the Land!" is the secular version of "This is the Word of the Lord." For most pro-abortion people, legality is the equivalent of morality. What is right or wrong is whatever the courts decide. In fact, former Supreme Court Justice Holmes said just this: "Right and wrong is the decision of the courts." The black-robed justices are awarded by many people an aura of infallibility. Another former Supreme Court justice, Robert Jackson, once remarked about the Court: "We are not final because we are infallible; we are infallible because we are final." Their track record, however, does not confirm either infallibility or finality.

A case in point: In 1856-57, the Dred Scott case—a remarkable parallel to the abortion (*Roe* v. *Wade* and *Doe* v. *Bolton*) cases—was argued before the United States Supreme Court. The Dred Scott case was concerned with the status of black Americans in the federal territories. In 1834, Dred Scott, a black slave and personal servant to Dr. John Emerson, a United States Army surgeon, was taken by his master from Missouri (a slave state) to Illinois (a free state) and from Illinois into the Wisconsin Territory, where slavery was prohibited. There Dred Scott married before returning with Dr. Emerson to Missouri in 1838. After Emerson's death, Scott sued (1846) Emerson's widow for his freedom and that of his wife and two children.

Eventually the case reached the United States Supreme Court. In this case of *Scott v. Sandford,* the Supreme Court decided that Congress had no power to prohibit slavery in the territories. Chief Justice Roger B. Taney delivered the Court's opinion that the Missouri Compromise prohibiting slavery was unconstitutional. In the majority opinion, three justices also held that a black person "whose ancestors were sold as slaves . . . was *not* entitled to the rights of a federal citizen and therefore had no standing in court" (italics added). What the Court was saying is that the black man is property, not a person.

Many competent lawyers see a remarkable parallel between this judgment of the Supreme Court and the abortion decision. Two of the justices in the Roger Taney Supreme Court strongly opposed slavery and considered it unconstitutional. However, the majority ruled that the prohibition of slavery was unconstitutional. Two of the justices in the Warren Burger Court dissented from the abortion decision. However, the Court ruled that all state laws in any way prohibiting an abortion were unconstitutional.

The biological evidence that black people are indeed human beings was obvious and available to the Taney Court. The biological evidence is conclusive that the fetus, the baby which has been conceived, is indeed a human being. Our country and our Constitution are committed to the right of every human being to life, liberty, and the pursuit of happiness.

The only way the Taney Court could have arrived at its conclusion about slavery was by making the basis of decision the color of one's skin. The only way the Burger Court could legalize the killing of millions of babies was by making the basis of decision the size and dependent condition of the fetus. The Taney Court deprived black people of protection by the law. The Burger Court did the same thing to preborn babies. It deprived them of their status as human beings, deprived them of all title to personhood and protection of the law. It conceded to them only "potential" life, a ridiculous term which no biologist would use.

Law professor Charles E. Rice, in his book *Beyond Abortion: The Theory and Practice of the Secular State* (Franciscan Herald Press, 1979), writes:

> The Supreme Court turned away from this developing line of cases [legal precedents affirming the personhood of the unborn] and, in holding that the unborn child is a nonperson, adopted the theory of the Dred Scott case, where in 1857 the Supreme Court held that the free descendants of slaves could not be citizens and said that slaves were property rather than persons. The framers of the Fourteenth Amendment clearly intended to reverse Dred Scott by ensuring that all human beings would be treated as persons. But the Supreme Court, in the 1973 rulings, chose instead the rationale used for the Nazis' extermination of the Jews: that an innocent human being can be declared a nonperson and deprived of life if his existence is inconvenient to others or if those others consider him unfit to live.

> The Court itself acknowledged in a footnote . . . that if the personhood of the unborn child were established, abortion could not be allowed, even to save the life of the mother. However, the Court solved

this problem by defining the unborn child as a nonperson. Therefore he has no rights.

So I am less than enthusiastic about the gospel of the Supreme Court when it is sanctimoniously preached as the law of the land. The Supreme Court is mandated to interpret the Constitution, to tell us what the Constitution says. In the Dred Scott and abortion decisions, I am convinced that the Court made the Constitution say what they wanted it to say, for pragmatic reasons.

In the beginning there was only a handful of activist Americans, convinced that the abolition of slavery was the only moral course for a country committed to the life, liberty, and pursuit of happiness of every human being. This handful stood firm, and history confirms their courageous victory. Slavery has been abolished. I am also convinced that a handful of loyal pro-life activists will persevere and that their courage will eventually be rewarded with the victory of life over death. If we cave in, the stones will rise to accuse us of unfaithfulness to the unborn, who have no voice of protest except ours.

"Never Let Them Say . . ."

Almost always, after a pro-life lecture or debate, someone would approach me with this remark: "Don't ever let them say that those babies are not wanted. We are childless, and we would love to have a child. But there are no babies available for adoption. They are all being destroyed." In fact, black markets for healthy, white babies are constantly being uncovered. In many places the going

107

price for a healthy white child is approximately five thousand dollars.

I have always felt a deep sympathy for couples who are unable to have children. Almost always, at the same time, I feel an unusual emotion: a sense of compassion for God, if that be possible. I am sure that as Father of us all, God wants all his children to have the fullness of life. Each of us is irreplaceable in his heart. If the Bible doesn't say that, it doesn't say anything. Later on we will take up the religious dimension of the abortion question. However, since it was so often repeated to me after pro-life talks, I wanted to include it here: "Never let them say that those babies aren't wanted!" I think there are a lot of people out there who want to embrace, love, and nourish the life that is now being destroyed.

"I have set before you life and death. . . . Therefore, choose life that you and your descendants may live" (Deuteronomy 30:19).

CHAPTER 8

DIALOGUE ABOUT DEATH
The Questions/The Answers

"To talk about the 'wanted' and the 'un-wanted' child smacks of bigotry and prejudice. Many of us have experienced the sting of being 'unwanted' by certain segments of our society. . . . One usually wants objects and if they turn out unsatisfactory, they are return-able. . . . Human beings are not returnable items."

—Grace Olivares, from
"Separate Statement," in
Population and the American Future:
The Report of the Commission on
Population Growth and the
American Future (p. 161)

The Questions They Asked

In the course of my tour on the pro-life circuit, I always welcomed questions and comments. Of course, there was a preponderance of questions from those sympathetic to my position. "What can I do?" they would ask. The unsympathetic questioner usually began with a life-related question which did not directly concern itself with abortion. For example, what do you think about war, prison reform, handgun control, world hunger, birth control? If my stance on one of these questions did not agree with that of the questioner, then he or she could at least argue that I was inconsistent.

Once the fact that a fetus is a living human being is established, there is no cogent argument with which to attack the anti-abortion position. I remember once a rather high-ranking officer in a church-related organization, who, obviously unhappy with my condemnation of abortion, asked my position concerning war. After describing my own qualified pacifism, I conceded that there probably is such a thing as a "just war." I added that the war against Hitler probably fulfilled the conditions for such a war. I was told rather haughtily that the "just war theory is medieval," and that I was proposing a "curious theology and a Mickey Mouse morality." I strongly suspect that the man really wanted to disagree with me about abortion. But how does a believer question the biblical commandment "Thou shall not kill!" especially in light of the fact that more human beings have been killed by abortion than in all the wars of all times? In such a context, direct attack on the anti-abortion stance is very difficult.

There were, however, some questions which bore more directly on the question of abortion. I would like to review them here, along with my responses. I would like to remind you that the assumption on which all of my answers were based is that the fetus is a living human being. I regard this as a scientifically established fact.

Question #1: In seeking a Human Life Amendment to the Constitution, which would outlaw abortion, are you not trying to impose your conscience on everyone?

My response: An act of conscience, we know, is the judgment that an individual makes about the morality of a given act or state. In the light of this definition of conscience as a judgment, my first urge, in the face of this question, was always to point out that the judgment of someone else is imposed on more than one and a half million babies each year. It is a judgment that for the baby is a death sentence. More than four thousand babies perish each day in this country because others have judged that they were unwanted and disposable.

However, I found that it was more effective to invoke the old Irish privilege of answering a question by asking one: If the lady next door were killing off her "born" children, on the grounds that she believed in conscience that this was the best thing for them, would you try to stop her? Would you at least notify the police? Or would you simply say that this was a matter of conscience and that you wouldn't impose your own beliefs or conscience? Not long ago a man in England, called the "Yorkshire Ripper," maintained that he was ordered by God to kill prostitutes. It was, he maintained in court, a matter of conscience. Had you known of his identity and activities, would you have tried to stop him? Or would you rather have conceded that it is a private matter of personal conscience?

Obviously, the right of conscience has its limits. You can swing your fist as much as you want, but your right to swing your fist ends at the tip of my nose. My rights do not preempt the rights of another. Abortion is not a matter of private morality. The rights and life of a weak and voiceless human being are at stake. The pro-life struggle is not to impose one's conscience on another but to preserve the right to life that is violated in every abortion.

Furthermore, according to present U.S. laws our right of conscience does not include mutilating or killing ourselves. Were one of us actively suicidal, he or she could be apprehended and kept in restraints until the suicidal urge was under control. Certainly no right of conscience can allow anyone to take the life of another innocent human being. And the preborn babies are just that: innocent human beings.

In a statement dated July 9, 1971, Rabbi David B. Hollander, former vice-president of the Rabbinical Alliance of America, said:

> Judaism, except where it is necessary to save the life of the mother, strongly prohibits abortion and places it in the category of the taking of human life, however "noble" the motivation. Even those who say that while they oppose abortion, they feel it is a private matter and the law should not interfere, are

simply not facing the fact that *the law always does and should interfere where human life is the issue.* Thus, the law forbids suicide, refusal to submit to medical treatment, or the mistreatment of children, the sick, and the helpless. The law forbids the abandonment of children by parents. Is there a greater "abandonment" than abortion? [italics added]

The United Nations, in its Declaration of the Rights of the Child, has decreed:

. . . the child, by reason of his physical and mental immaturity, needs special safeguards and care, including appropriate legal protection, *before as well as after birth.*

Question #2: Do you want women to go back to "the butchers," to back-alley and "coat-hanger abortions"?

My response: There are many possible responses to this question. One could quote statistics on maternal deaths. Before abortion was legalized there were perhaps several hundred such deaths each year in our country. An estimate, published by the Bureau of Vital Statistics of the U.S. Public Health Service, indicates that there were fewer than two hundred maternal deaths a year from illegal abortions in the United States in the late 1960s. Since abortion was legalized in this country there have been one and a half million infant deaths each year, and that number is growing.

In answering this question, one should also point out that legalized abortion probably does not reduce the number of illegal abortions. Drs. Hilgers and Shearin of the Mayo Clinic discovered that when permissive abortion laws were passed in eight European countries, the number of illegal abortions stayed about the same. In two countries, the number of illegal abortions actually increased. (Thomas Hilgers, *Induced Abortion: A Documented Report*, 2nd ed., Minnesota Citizens Concern for Life, 1973, Chap. 7) This is not as astounding as it might seem. The very same factor that leads many women to seek an abortion when it's illegal—the fear of disclosure that she's pregnant—still exists after abortion has been legalized and controlled through established medical institutions. (Cf. *Handbook on Abortion* by Dr. and Mrs. J. C. Willke, rev. ed., Hayes Publishing, 1975.)

Personally I feel a deep and sympathetic commitment to the many women who are troubled with unwanted pregnancies. I have counseled many such women and assisted them through their pregnancies. I have even held the hand of one young woman during her delivery. (Quite an experience!) I also feel a deep and gentle compassion for women who have aborted their babies. I have tried very hard to help those who have come to me with grinding remorse to find peace and forgiveness.

But when one mentions abortion, there are *two* human beings involved, *not just one,* the woman troubled with an unwanted pregnancy. There is another tiny human being who has no voice as yet to demand its rights, to plead for its life. The genetic package of the baby is complete. The genetic programming is already determined: eye color, hair color, blood type, bone structure, and much more. The cells are multiplying; growth has begun. The baby is a living, growing human being. Each stage of development from fertilization to old age is merely a process of maturation, which is obvious from the very beginning. Being born changes only the baby's dining habits, source of oxygen, and visibility. A journey of one thousand miles must begin with a single step.

Dr. Bernard Nathanson once speculated: "If the abdominal wall of the pregnant woman were transparent, what kind of abortion laws might we have?" (*Aborting America*, p. 211) Abortion is a hidden holocaust as well as a silent holocaust. If only the baby could be seen and could cry out for its life; but it has no voice and no visibility except ours.

Dr. Albert W. Liley is known as the "Father of Fetology." He is a world-renowned research professor in perinatal physiology at the National Women's Hospital in Auckland, New Zealand. His contribution to fetology has been monumental. It was he who perfected the process of intrauterine transfusion. He writes:

> In a world in which adults control power and purse, the fetus is at a disadvantage being small, naked and nameless and voiceless. He has no one except sympathetic adults to speak up for him and defend him— and equally no one except callous adults to condemn and attack him. Biologically, at no stage can we subscribe to the view that the fetus is merely an appendage of the mother. Genetically, mother and baby are separate individuals from conception. Physiologically, we must accept that the conceptus is, in the very large measure, in charge of the pregnancy, in command of his own environment and destiny with a tenacious purpose. . . . One hour after the sperm has penetrated the ovum, the nuclei of the two cells have fused and the genetic instructions from one parent have met the complementary instructions from the other parent to establish a whole design, the inheritance of a new person.

To return to the question about the "butcher shops" and "coat-hanger abortions": No, of course not. I don't want the mother (she *is* already a mother) to hurt herself or to be hurt in the act of destroying the life inside her. But my sympathy for her doesn't carry me to the point that I would set up an hygienic "killing center," where the child can be killed with surgical precision in antiseptic circumstances. As the late, great governor of Connecticut, Ella Grasso, once remarked: "Let us not kill the children of the poor, and then tell them how we have helped them."

I myself could never say: "Admittedly the poor woman has a problem, so let's make it safe for her and legally permissible for her to kill her child." This would certainly be a subhuman and dehumanizing logic. Such a lopsided sympathy and ethic would eventually dehumanize all of us. The real casualty would be our own humanity, our own civilization. Of course, we must do everything in our power to help the woman burdened with an unwanted or difficult pregnancy. However, let there be no human sacrifices on our altars, beseeching the great gods of science to create for us a pain-free world.

As the great woman to whom the Nobel Peace Prize was awarded, Mother Teresa of Calcutta, has said:

> To me, the nations with legalized abortions are the poorest nations. The great destroyer of peace today is the crime against the innocent unborn child.

Question #3: In the matter of abortion, shouldn't a woman be allowed to make a choice for herself? Doesn't a woman have a right over her own body?

My response: Of course, we should all have the liberty to make our own choices. However, most of our choices are social, that is, they affect others. Abortion obviously affects another. Even though a woman's right over her own body is limited, as indicated earlier in the discussion of self-multilation and suicide, this choice regarding abortion concerns not only her own body but also the body and the life of her child.

Dr. Margaret White, British magistrate and physician, told a Illinois Right to Life and Birthright Benefit in Chicago on November 2, 1974:

> You know, I often wish we still used the old-fashioned language for pregnant women. When my mother became pregnant, they said, "She is with child." If we use that way of speaking a bit more often, people might realize what they're doing when they are destroying that child.

Very often when I heard this question, I saw it rising out of a feminist context. It seems to interpret an anti-abortion mentality as an anti-feminist mentality. On the contrary, I am convinced that abortion is fundamentally anti-woman as well as anti-child. Of course, half of the children killed in abortions are female, but that is not the main point. I think that we have here in our country a structure which exploits women, urging them to have abortions as the "convenient" or "sensible" thing to do. Having an abortion is presented in this social-legal structure as a symbol of female liberation. Women are assured that it is just a simple procedure. Francis X. Meehan wrote about this deception in a pamphlet entitled *Pro-Life Work and Social Justice* (National Conference of Catholic Bishops' Committee for Pro-Life Activities, 1980):

. . . when one moment a woman is going to have a baby and the next moment is not, any structure which tries to make "terminating pregnancy" sound like a simple procedure is telling a social lie. Yes, the technique may be simple, but the reality of what the technique accomplishes is not. . . .

The atmosphere in which abortion thrives is the product of a male system. It enforces male hegemony [domination] over human sexuality and human life. The woman is still property. Now she can be treated as property with greater impunity than before. She is forced to breathe in this ideology of "property." She treats herself as property; she even treats the child of her womb, flesh of her flesh, as property. The male has won again. The woman undergoes double jeopardy. The system is not around after the abortion to help the woman handle her feelings of alienation. She is merely dismissed from the clinic—after paying the fee, of course.

. . . It is not pro-woman to seduce young women away from real choices, to prevent them from making choices which do no violence to their own bodies and the bodies of their children when they are "with child." [p. 6]

Question #4: There is a new medical procedure called amniocentesis. A sample of amniotic fluid, containing sloughed-off cells from the body of the baby, can be drawn off, cultured, and studied. By this process sickness and/or abnormality in the infant can sometimes be diagnosed before birth. If the process does indicate sickness or abnormality, wouldn't it be better for the mother to have an abortion in this case?

My response: First, it should be established that this procedure is possible only after the child has entered the fourth month of life. By this time all the physical systems of the child—the brain, the heart, the kidneys, and so forth—are functioning. The New York Medical Association has declared that by this time an abortion becomes "fraught with tremendous danger." It would actually be safer for the mother to let the baby come to term, be delivered normally, and then be killed. The baby would be just as dead if it were killed in the ninth month of life as it would be if killed in the fourth month of life. Most people would find this logical, practical, and utilitarian solution very hard to stomach. It sounds callous, but it does underline the fact that the child, because it is imperfect, is not being considered at all. The only consideration is given to the mother, to her health and her convenience.

My own response to the question of deformity or retardation in the infant is that of Dr. Rosenblum, already quoted. Do you believe in love? Love does not discriminate: "I will love you only if you are perfect. We do not tolerate imperfect human beings that might prove burdensome."

Love says: "Baby, we are going to love you. We will make arms for you. We will be your arms. We will take care of you. You are one of us, a member of our family. We will always love you."

Pearl S. Buck, the famous author, wrote the Foreword to *The Terrible Choice,* a book based on the proceedings of the International Conference on Abortion sponsored by the Harvard Divinity School and the Joseph P. Kennedy Jr. Foundation. In it she writes:

> As the mother of a child retarded from phenylketonuria, I can ask myself . . . could it have been possible for me to have had foreknowledge of her thwarted life, would I have wanted abortion? . . .

No, I would not. . . . My child's life has not been meaningless. She has indeed brought comfort and practical help to many people who are parents of retarded children or are themselves handicapped. Even though gravely retarded it has been worthwhile for her to have lived. [pp. x-xi]

Question #5: Would you allow an abortion in the cases of rape and incest?

My response: Pregnancy from rape or incest is extremely rare, especially if the victim goes immediately to a hospital. I think it is important to establish that we are talking about a very small number of cases. However, the possibility is there, and so the question must be asked. From a legal viewpoint, if we had a law that permitted abortions in cases of rape and incest only, it would be almost impossible to establish or to deny any claim that a pregnancy resulted from rape or incestuous relations. For this reason, English law (less permissive than our own) does not even mention rape as grounds for an abortion.

From an ethical point of view, however, the baby is conceived, and that baby remains an innocent human being. Let's consider the alternatives. (1) If we have the baby killed by abortion, it certainly does not help the baby. In the short run it may well relieve the mother of a traumatic burden, but it will leave her with a lifelong memory of having once carried a child which she had destroyed. Today's experiences are tomorrow's memories. In general, the experience of abortion is a long and painful memory. (2) In the second alternative, the mother is given all the support and assistance that counseling and loving concern can offer. She is helped to new heights of courage and respect for human life. The baby is allowed to live and is, after delivery, offered for adoption. ("Don't ever let them tell you that those babies are not wanted. We are childless and would love to have an adopted child.") The mother, in this alternative, lives with the memory of her courageous and generous commitment to life.

I have personally helped one young girl through such a pregnancy and delivery of a baby conceived in a situation very close to rape. After her baby was offered for adoption and welcomed into the arms and hearts of the adoptive parents, the young woman and I looked back together on the experience. I asked her for her thoughts and feelings. Her answer was: "Oh, I'm a much better, braver person. As that baby grew inside me, I think I grew up. Even though I still have some bitterness toward the baby's father that I must work through, I still delight in the thought that the baby is alive, gurgling and smiling up into the faces of his adoptive parents." Yesterday's experiences are today's memories.

Question #6: Isn't having an abortion better than having an unwanted child?

My response: "Being wanted" is a phrase that implies having value for someone else. The implication of the question is that the baby has no value in itself; its being wanted constitutes its value. During a recent presidential election campaign, the abortion issue surfaced as a key issue, although both candidates declared their personal opposition to abortion. During the campaign, many people were asked for their opinion of abortion. As part of the local television coverage of the election in my city (Chicago), a spokeswoman for the Planned Parenthood Federation said: "We in Planned Parenthood believe that every child who is conceived has the right to be born if it is wanted." As the saying goes, " . . . and that's all she wrote." She did not say, but it does not require a Rhodes scholar to deduce what was left unsaid: " . . . and if the baby is not wanted, it should be killed." The logic is that my wanting you to live is what confers upon you your human worth, your respectability as a person.

This is not to deny that there are situations in which a mother can conceive a child when she does not want a child or at least does not want another child. It is certainly understandable that, in a given case, a woman might not want a child because of her health or life situation. We would certainly offer such a woman compassion, under- standing, and love. However, it must be emphat- ically denied that it is this wanting or not wanting the child that makes the child worthwhile or worthless.

Also, we must not delude ourselves that we are helping a woman when we enable her to make the decision to have her baby killed. We are certainly not helping her to be a better person because abortion is a dehumanizing decision and a long and painful memory. Dr. Eloise Jones, a Toronto psychiatrist, explained why she has stopped refer- ring women for abortions.

An abortion has not helped the self-image of any woman I have talked with. I was listening to one recently. She was very frightened lest her teenage daughter discover what she had done, and since the abortion she has become increasingly fearful, hostile

and unresponsive to her husband. In her and in others I have been presented with psychosomatic illness . . . all kinds of neurotic disturbances and some deep depressive reactions.

There are and there should be humane, compassionate organizations like Birthright and Heartbeat, which provide counseling and other forms of assistance to women who are pregnant in difficult circumstances. I have personally been connected with Birthright for more than five years. I must say that I am deeply impressed with the compassion and kindness of the women and the men in this organization, founded by Louise Summerhill. Their unselfish and loving dedication is a strong affirmation of human worth: both the mother's worth and the child's worth.

There is also an organization called Alternatives to Abortion International. In a letter published in the January, 1975, issue of their publication entitled *Heartbeat*, the directors wrote:

Nothing is more crucial than making available to [the pregnant woman] the positive alternatives for life as weighed against the negative and destructive ones of abortion. Because she has a personal problem, her needs can only be met individually, on a one-to-one basis through someone who cares about her and her baby. . . . The more positive, personal, and practically helpful the assistance, the less likely will she elect abortion. [p. 237]

Finally, Pope John Paul II told a group of pilgrims in Rome on January 3, 1979:

The pregnant mother must not be left alone, left alone with her doubts, her difficulties, her temptations. We must stand with her, so that she might have the necessary courage and faith, so that her conscience will not be burdened. . . . Everyone must in a certain way be with every mother who is to give birth and offer her every possible aid. [Religious News Service]

In trying to redress the imbalance of the pro-abortionists whose only concern is given to the pregnant mother, we must not fall into the opposite error, and give all our concern only to the unborn child. It is critical to the credibility of the pro-life position that the pregnant woman be cared for and attended with the same compassion as that given to the preborn baby. Just as the voiceless baby needs the protection of the human family, so too does the troubled and burdened woman who faces the problems of an unwanted pregnancy. Both the preborn child and the mother need all the protection and help which the rest of us can offer. To speak for and to help one and not the other is totally inconsistent with the basic pro-life tenet that each and every human life has absolute value.

In a related area, child abuse, it was for a long time asserted in the pro-abortion propaganda that child abuse was the result of people having "unwanted children." However, studies have proved just the opposite. In one study made at the University of Southern California Medical Center, the department of pediatrics, it was discovered that over 90 percent of battered and abused children were the result of planned pregnancies. Furthermore, it should be noted that since the abortion decision of the Supreme Court, child abuse has become epidemic in this country.

In fact, Dr. Bernard Farber, a sociologist from Arizona State University, sees abortion and child abuse going hand in hand in modern American society. Statistics certainly must be embarrassing to the pro-abortion propagandists who have been insisting that as abortion increases child abuse will decrease. Dr. Farber says that just the reverse is true and that children themselves are considered to have less value for modern life.

Dr. John Fletcher of the Genetic Research Group at the Institute of Society, Ethics and the Life Sciences, Hastings Center, made a study of couples seeking genetic counseling. He is quoted in the September, 1975, issue of *Psychology Today* as saying: "To contemplate the death of your baby in the third month of pregnancy changes very seriously the attitude we, as a society, usually have toward our babies" (p. 22). And Dr. Vincent Fontana, chairman of the New York City Mayor's Task Force on Child Abuse and Neglect, says in his book *Somewhere a Child Is Crying* (Macmillan, 1973):

> It is unfair, uninformed, and, I believe, dangerous, to preach the doctrine that abused and neglected children are unwanted children and to imply that unplanned or unwanted children are going to be maltreated. The assumption that every battered child is an unwanted child, or that most or even a large proportion of abused children are unwanted children, is totally false. [p. 239]

Dr. Farber, in an interview with the Phoenix newspaper *Arizona Republic,* said that, as the abortion mentality breaks down family structures, there is "less commitment to families [and so] there will be more criminal action—child abuse, family disputes, aggressive acts toward competitors or rivals and stealing from spouses or parents."

Princeton ethicist Paul Ramsey wonders why we are so surprised at the new epidemic of child abuse. Obviously there is a connection, he points out, between what we can do to a baby in the first nine months of life and thereafter.

The Supreme Court of West Germany, in its February, 1975, decision banning abortion-on-demand during the first twelve weeks of pregnancy, stated: "We cannot ignore the educational impact of abortion on the respect for life." The Court was aware that what could happen to the fetus before birth might well have an effect on how the baby was treated after birth. In his book *Death Before Birth* (Thomas Nelson, 1977), Protestant theologian Harold O. J. Brown observes that parents might, at least subconsciously, reason: "I didn't have to have him. I could have killed him before he was born. So if I knock him around a little now that he is born, isn't that my perfect right?"

CHAPTER 9

TWO DIFFERENT WORLDS
The Old Ethic
The New Ethic

"To have destroyed the defective infant, Helen Keller, would have been to destroy also the teacher-humanitarian who was Anne Sullivan. In countless cases throughout the world a defective child has not been an expensive, heart-rending burden but a priceless gift that has brought out the hidden strengths of a father, a mother and sisters and brothers. . . . How foolish that we condemn the 'Me-Generation' and then are tempted to remove from them the defective children who offer them the opportunity to forget the me and to remember the others. . . . We will never know how many Helen Kellers and Beethovens are destroyed each year in America's abortion mills, or how many Anne Sullivans are left without the challenge that makes an Anne Sullivan. We climb a mountain because it is there and calls us. We solve a problem because it is there and challenges us. How terrible if someone leveled all the mountains and removed all the problems. How little opportunity would be left for human beings to become both really human and really Godlike."

—Father George Tribou,
    educator, Little Rock, Arkansas,
    from an unpublished speech,
    January 31, 1980

Two Different Worlds

The kind of world we live in is governed to a large extent by the consensus ethic of that world. It's something like a game: There have to be rules upon which everyone agrees. As we have been saying, there are two ethics competing for domination in our contemporary American society. There is the traditional, humane pro-life ethic, which sees every human life as valuable in itself. It offers loving acceptance and care to every human being, without distinction of size, shape, skin color, or self-sufficiency. It assumes that every life is worth living.

Under this ethic, everyone who comes into this world comes as a part of our human family. Everyone comes to us as a unique and unrepeatable gift. There will be, in this world, people like the late Helen Keller: deaf and blind and unable to communicate until "Annie" Sullivan comes along. Anne Sullivan will attain the stature of a tremendous human being only because there is the challenge of a Helen Keller to call greatness out of her. You climb the mountain because it is there. There will also be in this world retarded and deformed people. There will be schools for "exceptional children" and "Special Olympics."

There will be sympathetic and compassionate treatment of the aged and the senile, who are also a part of our family and who motivate us to be human and loving. The message that the aged deliver will be a request, an invitation, and a challenge to our capacity for love and endurance. When we rise to this challenge, like muscles that grow strong with exercise, our societal capacity for mutual love and concern will also grow. We will become more and more humane toward one another. The handicapped and the aged are here as much for us, perhaps, as for themselves. Like Anne Sullivan we can really become great human beings if we choose to love them, not to kill them. The world under the pro-life ethic may not be as neat and clean and pain-free as the world ruled by a quality-of-life ethic, but it is far more humane and compassionate and a much more loving world.

Eunice Kennedy Shriver, writing in the April, 1968, *McCalls* Magazine, describes a world which has truly accepted the pro-life ethic.

> Instead of becoming the Hard Society we could become a just and compassionate one. Instead of destroying life, we could destroy the conditions that make life intolerable. In this society, every child, regardless of his capacities or the circumstances of his birth, would be welcomed, loved, and cared for—and abortion would cease to preoccupy us, because it would not be necessary. [p. 140]

Struggling to replace this pro-life ethic is the quality-of-life ethic. This ethic is pragmatic and utilitarian. It does not attach absolute value to any human life in itself. Rather it sets "a standard of quality" which every individual life must meet; if a given life fails to meet this standard, it becomes disposable and will be rejected.

In *Pediatric Nursing* for July/August, 1976, Richard E. Harbin, of the Hawley Army Hospital at Fort Harrison in Indiana, promotes and describes the New Ethic. He quotes English novelist Henry Fielding to the effect that "it hath been often said that it is not death, but dying, which is terrible." Harbin argues that medical personnel must be

ready to counsel death when, in difficult cases, the question is posed, "What would you do if it were your baby?" Harbin writes:

> Decisions are easily made for those who profess that the sanctity of life is the overriding consideration in every case. There is no decision with such a code—all infants must be afforded the greatest attempts to salvage their lives, regardless of life quality or the costs emotionally or financially to the family and society.
>
> . . . As medical technology has advanced, so must medical ethics. The traditional ethics based on the sanctity of life must now give way to a code of ethics of the quality of life. . . . None will deny that decisions can become morally confusing and difficult, but for our own sake and that of generations to come we must not shirk this task. It is our duty to see that the development of medical ethics keeps in step with scientific developments.

In this world, living by the New Ethic, those in control will decide which lives are wanted because of their quality of excellence and their ability to contribute to the quality of life in general. The parameters are vague but negotiable. We have already seen the proposal by two Nobel Prize-winning scientists that no person or human life be protected by law for the first three days after birth or until it passes certain tests. This will enable a physician to pronounce definitively on the quality and perfection of the baby, and to make a life-or-death decision. We have heard one of these Nobel Prize winners recommend compulsory death for everyone at age eighty. It is the quality of life which is paramount, and supposedly high quality does not survive past eighty years.

We have also seen the proposal of a Wisconsin

state legislator that everyone be legally enabled to appoint another to kill him/herself, providing the person who does the killing is fourteen years of age or older. We have heard seventeen out of twenty medical personnel say that they could see no moral objection to killing a self-sustaining child if the quality of that child's life is not up to standards set by those in control. We have also seen a medical proposal that Down's syndrome children be used for medical experimentation "because they make no other contribution to society."

A world shaped by the quality-of-life ethic shuns on principle all suffering and immediately anesthetizes all pain. By consensus agreement, it forbids anyone to be a burden, under pain of death. It puts your life in my hands, if I am in control, and my life in your hands, if you are in control.

Dr. R. A. Gallop of the University of Manitoba, Winnipeg, Canada, writes:

> Once you permit the killing of the unborn child, there will be no stopping. There will be no age limit. You are setting off a chain reaction that will eventually make you the victim.
>
> Your children will kill you because you permitted the killing of their brothers and sisters. Your children will kill you because they will not want to support you in your old age. Your children will kill you for your homes and estates.
>
> If a doctor will take money for killing the innocent in the womb, he will kill you with a needle when paid by your children. This is the terrible nightmare you are creating for the future.

The New Ethic would knowingly and willingly lay its human sacrifices on the altar of "quality existence" to insure the creation of a true master race, just like the one Hitler envisioned and hoped to produce in his dreams for the Third Reich. All the mountains would be leveled. All the problem persons would be removed. No calls, no challenges to human greatness or to unselfish love. Just a perfect, loveless world for perfect, unloving persons. Infants would understandably tremble during physical examination, and the aged would be reluctant to drink a glass of water handed to them by their children.

From Personal Experience:
Hospital Chaplaincy

There are two very personal chapters of my life I would like to share with you at this point. Both experiences have helped me to understand the difference between the two ethics and the two different worlds that each would create. During my long (fourteen years) training as a Jesuit, I read thousands of books, wrote hundreds of papers, accumulated a handful of academic degrees. During this prolonged period of Jesuit formation, all the emphases were academic. All scenes of suffering, the blood and guts of life, were screened out of sight. The sick went to a hospital and came home either with regained health or in a flower-bedecked coffin. The wailing of the newborn and the gasping of the dying were quarantined out of our existence. Then came the hospital chaplaincy in Akron, Ohio. This was the place and time of my life-transforming experience in witnessing the birth of a baby.

As mentioned earlier, my first thought on entering the hospital was: "I've never seen anyone die. I've never seen anyone covered with blood. I've never seen anyone born. This is going to be an initiation into life." It was my understatement of that year. There was the boy who was burned to death in the flaming wreckage of his car, and the girl who killed herself with a gun in her mouth and a bullet through her brain. I remember vividly a teenage girl clutching the corpse of her mother, pleading with her mother to "come back." Also there was a young wife waving her hand in front of her face, trying to erase the unexpected news of her husband's sudden death. There was an anorexic girl trying to starve herself to death. There were bloody victims of car accidents in various states of consciousness. The phone next to my bed in the middle of almost every night jangled me awake with the news that "A patient is expiring!"

There was both birth and death, grief and rejoicing: the whole gamut of the agonies and ecstasies of human existence. Near the end of my tour of duty as a chaplain, my head ached as it tried to find a place inside for the sudden rush of new life experiences. What I really want to say to you at this point is that this was the most educational time and the most maturing experience of my life. I learned more about what it means to be a human being during this time than at any other time of my life.

Of course, the Jesuit training is much changed now. (I am in middle age: the years between Ovaltine and Geritol.) Today the Jesuit formation includes much experience with the struggling, the hungering, the bleeding, the living and the dying of other human beings. Our young Jesuits receive, as an essential part of their training, much more direct experience with the joys and sorrows, the gore and the glory of human existence. The quality-of-life ethic would "spare" us the most humanizing of our human experiences.

Just as a journey of a thousand miles must begin with a single step, so does a societal ethic begin with a single premise. In the quality-of-life ethic, this premise would be: "It is not a human life in itself that is important. What is important is the quality of that life. There are lives not worth living. Lives that have been adjudged meaningful and wanted should be allowed to continue; all other lives should be ended." Consequently, the test for the unborn is whether they are "physically perfect" and "wanted."

I try to imagine a world created by the logical extensions of this quality-of-life ethic. It is a world that will answer no challenges, will abide no struggle, and will tolerate no one unless his/her life and contribution to society are considered meaningful and worthwhile. It is a world completely streamlined so that we who are fit and productive, as long as we remain fit and productive, can soar through it with the maximum amount of pleasure and a minimum amount of struggle and pain. In this world there are no calls to human, interpersonal greatness. The Helen Kellers of this world are dispatched promptly. The Anne Sullivans have no mountains to climb. There are no invitations to break the fixation with ourselves and to learn the meaning of unselfish love. We eliminate such invitations. To all those with mental or physical handicaps who would come among us we would refuse all hospitality. We would grant them no citizenship in our world or membership in our family.

We would say to the physically handicapped, to the mentally retarded, to the aged and senile: "No! We don't want you. There is no place in our world for you. We are a super race. We don't tolerate imperfection in our world. The rejection of you will improve the quality of life for all the rest of us. We won't hear your message and we will not listen to your song. We don't want your love and we don't want to give you ours. You would be a burden, and so you must die."

Oh, God! What an awful, cold, and heartless world. What a dehumanized existence brought on by people meaning to be humanitarian in their motivation. As Maria Montessori wrote in *The Secret of Childhood* (Ballantine, 1972): "We have an instinctive tendency to mask our sins by protestations of lofty and necessary duties." Is anyone there? Does anyone see what I see? Does anyone care?

I am convinced that we are moving closer to this abhorrent, dehumanizing world. I see our country at the crossroads of decision. We are being pushed by the judicial system, by the media, by many scientists, by the pleasure seekers and the power brokers to make the world more comfortable for ourselves, to accept the New Ethic. The euphemisms and the propaganda are like a sweet mask of anesthesia, dulling our sensitivities to the killing, focusing our eyes on the dangling delights of a pain-free world of perfect people.

I remember seeing a German movie called *I Accuse*, which was part of the Nazi propaganda for euthanasia. Dr. Leo Alexander mentions it in his article on the New Ethic from which we have quoted. Of this motion picture Dr. Alexander writes:

> This film depicts the life history of a woman suffering from multiple sclerosis; in it her husband, a doctor, finally kills her to the accompaniment of soft piano music rendered by a sympathetic colleague in an adjoining room. Acceptance of this ideology was implanted even in the children. [p. 39]

It is, indeed, a time of national clarification of values. The dramatic and stunning accomplishments of science have brought us to a new moment of decision in which we will either affirm our traditional respect for the sanctity of every life or accept the utilitarian ethic which promises to raise the quality of life for those of us who remain. As I think I learned from my seminary training and hospital chaplaincy experience, our humanity requires contact with the basic experiences of birth, suffering, struggling, bleeding, and dying. Our generosity and capacity for loving need to be challenged. To eliminate all the scenes of suffering and to reject all the challenges of generosity and love, as the New Ethic would promise to do, the real loss would be of our own humanity, our human greatness.

From Personal Experience: The Legacy of My Mother's Life

There is a second deeply personal experience I would like to share with you. In the ten years before my mother's death in 1976, we became very close. Our communication was profound; our sharing and mutual understanding grew to be very beautiful. During these ten years my mother was for the most part bedridden, almost totally crippled with arthritis, troubled with congestive heart failure which resulted in many brushes with death. There were even sporadic periods in which my mother seemed to pass in and out of the clouds of senility.

Once, near the end of her life, I confided to her that I had discovered in myself a real fear of death. I explained my own understanding of this fear, namely that I saw death as "the moment of naked truth" when we will be stripped of all our pretenses and posturing. I see death as the moment when we will meet God and be completely penetrated by his gaze. And we will be judged not by the words in our mouths but by the love in our hearts. For me, at the time, death seemed like the final examination of the heart.

I can still see my dear, bedridden mother, as she turned her head slowly on the pillow and looked at me with soft and sympathetic eyes. She said:

> I have never feared death since you children have been grown up. I didn't want to leave you before that, while you were still children. Now I have no fears of death. But John, do you know what I do fear? Pain. I have had so much pain with this miserable old arthritis, with the swelling in my feet and the struggle to breathe when my heart gets too weak. I think I have learned a lot and grown a lot because of the suffering. But I asked the Lord: "When you come for me, will you tiptoe in here and kiss me softly while I am sleeping?"

My mother was eighty-eight years old when she died . . . in her sleep, of course. The Lord who tiptoed in and kissed her softly while she was sleeping could refuse her nothing. The last twenty-four unconscious hours of her life I sat with her, holding her hands in mine. We waited together for the Angel of Death. During the time of waiting, I sat there remembering all that she had done for me. The touch of her gentle hands was so healing on the head of a sick child. Those hands had sewed so many clothes, cooked so many meals, made so many sandwiches and wrapped them in wax paper and put them in little brown bags for school. Those hands tied my first pair of shoes, bathed my body when I was a baby, rubbed Vicks on my chest when I had a cough, and put cool cloths on my forehead when I was nauseous. Her hands also spanked me when I needed spanking, and caressed me when I needed tenderness.

In those profoundly meaningful last hours of my mother's life, an angry thought suddenly interrupted my meditative count of blessings. Somewhere, out of the shadows of the night, came the thought that there were no doubt some (proponents of the New Ethic) who would say: "She's a vegetable. Give her an injection. After all, she's eighty-eight. She is only an expense now. Besides, what kind of meaningful life does she have!"

The thought infuriated me. I wanted to scream: "Don't you ever call my mother a vegetable! Once I was carried very lovingly in her body. Her gentle hands were my introduction to human warmth and love. Her melodious voice sang to me the first songs I ever heard. It was in her eyes that I first saw and found my own sense of worth. Don't you ever say that she is a vegetable. She is my mother, and we are waiting . . . waiting together for death."

If I had to pick out the most humanizing, maturing, and life-transforming days of my life, I would certainly have to include those last twenty-four hours of my mother's life. She was in a coma, breathing uneasily, waiting for the Lord to tiptoe in and kiss her softly while she was sleeping. I would dread a world that would reject such experiences. Converts to the New Ethic might well shake their heads at the futility of a tear-filled waiting for death when a simple injection could end it all. But what an impoverished life such logic would leave us. What impoverished human beings we would become.

The ten bedridden years of my mother's life were, from a human point of view, the richest in our relationship. I could at last do some little things for her because she could no longer do them for herself. It was most enriching to be able to make some return of love to someone who had loved me so long and so faithfully. In the twilight of her life, it seemed that she was at her finest. The experience of complete openness with each other introduced me to parts of myself that I didn't know existed, that I had never experienced before. I feel sure that my mother had a similar experience. What a terrible and personal loss I would have suffered if she had been "put out of her misery" because the supposedly meaningful and productive days of her life were over. The real victim of the New Ethic, if we should make that choice, will certainly be our own humanity. We will become the casualties of our own choice. We will regress into the cult of comfort in a world without mountains.

The Fork in the Road: Abortion

In the beginning of this book I offered my

opinion that our country was experiencing the "best of times, the worst of times," and certainly a time of national clarification of values. I think that we are at the "Day of Decision." I truly believe that whatever we decide on the abortion issue will by a very logical and inevitable progression become our decision between the Old Ethic of unconditional respect for life and the New Ethic which insists upon the quality of life and which respects the human right to life only after admission tests are taken and passed. Malcolm Muggeridge has called abortion "the slippery slope." His image is clear: Once we start down that hill, it is so slippery that we will be pushed along by the logic of the first accepted premise and there will be no stopping.

Dr. John Kelly, who left this country because he couldn't pretend to be an innocent bystander at mass murder, left behind a prophecy for the future. He knew that once we rationalize and legalize the killing of the unborn, there will be no stemming the tides of death. This is what Dr. Gallop was saying when he wrote, "Once you permit the killing of the unborn child, there will be no stopping. There will be no age limit. You are setting off a chain reaction that will eventually make you the victim." Once we take it upon ourselves to end the lives of four thousand innocent babies each day because they are not wanted, we have accepted not only abortion, but the principle that we can take an unwanted life. Of course, the New Ethic propagandists have no trouble with this. However, I am confident that in the end there will be enough of us who cannot live with this horror. We will no longer lay human sacrifices on

the altars of utility and the quality of life. We will no longer weigh human lives on the pan scales over against things, like money and convenience.

Abortion is clearly the top of the slippery slope. It is the fork in the road. Whatever we decide about this issue will by logical progression be our choice of ethic and the kind of world we will live in. I personally regret any argument against abortion that is based only on what abortion will lead to. Abortion in itself is the great tragedy. It is not wrong only because of what it will lead us to. It is a monstrous evil in itself. More than four thousand innocent lives are taken each day in this land of the free and home of the brave, whose lady holds high the torch of welcome to human life and invites the world:

> . . . Give me your tired, your poor,
> Your huddled masses yearning to breathe free,
> The wretched refuse of your teeming shore.
> Send these, the homeless, tempest-tost to me,
> I lift my lamp beside the golden door!

Still abortion, though it is a terrible tragedy in itself, is not the full tragedy. The fullness of tragedy will be completed only in the days and years to come when our humanity will be drowned in the tides and deluge of death.

In the January 23, 1971, issue of *Saturday Review*, former editor Norman Cousins deplored the increasing desensitization of this nation to violence, to the exploitation of sex, and to our decline of respect for life. He wrote:

> What is most damaging of all is that the process itself obscures what is happening, so that our highest responses are being blunted without our knowing it. [p. 31]

Abortion Procedures

The very procedures used in abortions are themselves shocking and repulsive. A brief description is included here, not to be sensational but simply to state the facts. There are basically five methods now in use. The first is called D & C, or dilation and curettage. The cervix, or mouth of the womb, is first stretched open. A curette, or sharp loop-shaped knife, is then inserted. As the walls of the uterus are scraped, the placenta and the unborn child are cut into pieces small enough to be scraped out or removed by forceps. In a suction-curettage abortion, a tube is inserted into the uterus, and the suction breaks and crushes the body parts of the baby and draws them out.

With both of these methods, the resulting tissue is clearly identifiable as small pieces of a baby. The actual cause of death is the physical dismemberment of the baby's body.

The third method is dilation and extraction (D & E), used after the twelfth week of pregnancy. It is a dismemberment procedure: The unborn child is cut into pieces, the larger body pieces are extracted, and the remainder is removed either by a D & C or suction-curettage. Sometimes it is necessary to crush the head of the baby before removal.

The fourth method is called saline injection. It is usually performed after the sixteenth week of pregnancy. A long needle is injected through the mother's abdomen to extract a certain amount of the amniotic fluid. This portion of the fluid is replaced with a toxic salt solution which burns the outer layers of the child's skin and poisons its system. An increase in movement is noted as the baby inhales and swallows the solution. The baby most often convulses, goes into a coma, and dies an hour or two later. Labor to expel the dead baby begins twenty-four to twenty-eight hours after this. In these first four procedures, the unborn child dies from mutilation or poisoning before it can be removed from the womb.

The fifth method, hysterotomy, is generally used only when saline injection is impractical. The baby is delivered as it would be in a Caesarian section. Almost all babies delivered by hysterotomy are born alive. Many cry and kick. Within a few minutes or hours, however, most die of exposure or neglect.

One of the euphemisms the pro-abortion propaganda has used to describe these processes is called "induced death." It is, of course, a euphemism for "killing." At any rate, the effect on the baby is the same: the baby is dead.

Experimentation on Aborted Babies

The Upjohn Pharmaceutical Company perfected Prostin F2 Alpha, one of a group of prostaglandin hormones, for use in abortions. When injected into a pregnant woman, it induces labor and delivery. In January, 1974, the Federal Drug Administration approved F2 Alpha for use during second-trimester abortions. Many physicians prefer this for, unlike other abortion procedures during which the baby is either mangled or burned, this method may often result in the delivery of an intact little body which is still alive and can be used for later experiments. Dr. Kurt Hirschhorn of New

York's Mount Sinai Hospital, one of many physicians engaged in "fetal research," has stated that, "with prostaglandins, you can arrange the whole abortion . . . so [the baby] comes out viable in the sense that it can survive hours or a day." (*National Observer,* April 21, 1973)

It is hardly a secret that there has been extensive experimentation done on the unborn because they have no protection of the law. The Supreme Court has declared them "nonpersons." According to *Arizona Republic* staff reporter Randy Collier, Drs. Robert Tamis, Mark Gross, and Robert Wechsler, all ob/gyns, were commissioned by E. R. Squibb and Sons (based in Princeton, N.J.) to test a hypertension drug on pregnant women who were planning on abortions "anyway." Squibb wanted to know the effects of the high-blood-pressure pills known as "Nadolol" on the unborn babies. After the abortions, two milliliters of blood were taken from each baby and sent to Squibb for analysis.

According to the report, the doctors got most of their patients from Maricopa County Hospital, offering a free abortion to the fourteen women who would submit themselves to four days of drug intake prior to their prostaglandin abortions. During the four days samples of amniotic fluid were extracted. According to veteran reporter Collier, all parties concerned have admitted to the arrangement. Squibb paid the abortion center ten thousand dollars. (*The Arizona Republic,* March 25, 1981)

In a March 3, 1975, article on abortion, *Newsweek* also pointed out that although prostaglandin abortions may be safer for the mother, "the fetus is more likely to be delivered alive." Infants aborted in this way are often sent to a hospital's pathology lab or anatomy department where they can be used for research purposes. Wilhamine Dick, testifying at the Sharp Abortion Law Commission Hearing on March 14, 1972, said that Pittsburgh's Magee Women's Hospital packed aborted babies in ice while they were still moving and shipped them to experimental labs.

Sometimes still showing signs of life, older infants have their organs removed or are given massive doses of medication for later study. According to the *Washington Post* (April 15, 1973), Dr. Gerald Gaull, chief of pediatrics at New York State Institute for Basic Research in Mental Retardation, "injects radioactive chemicals into umbilical cords of fetuses. . . . While the heart is still beating he removes their brains, lungs, liver and kidneys for study."

Also, the Connecticut attorney general presented an affidavit to the U.S. Supreme Court, March 14, 1973, regarding a Yale-New Haven experiment in which a baby was dissected without anesthesia before he died. And the *American Journal of Obstetrics and Gynecology* reported on May 15, 1974, a little over a year after the Supreme Court decision, that "the occasional delivery of a fetus with a heartbeat suggests that . . . [these] fetal tissues might be suitable for organ transplants . . . and for basic research."

Does all this sound as grisly and Nazi-like to you as it does to me? The Supreme Court decided that the unborn baby is a nonperson before the law. They are property, not persons. Disposable items. Many medical personnel seem to have accepted this definition literally and have treated the babies and their tiny bodies accordingly.

A new publication, *Medical Holocaust* by William Brennan (Nordland Publishing, 1980), offers conclusive factual information to link the modern abortion ethic with Nazi social policies in the years preceding World War II. Brennan's thesis focuses on the role played by the medical professionals— both German and American—in creating and directing the technology, the credibility, and even the legal sanctions which made possible the mass extermination programs.

Brennan writes: "Although every holocaust ever perpetrated is an unprecedented event in its own right, this should not detract from what all holocausts share in common . . . the systematic and widespread destruction of millions looked upon as indiscriminate masses of subhuman expendables." Brennan maintains that the necessary cultural environment for a human holocaust is present "whenever any society can be misled into defining individuals as less than human and therefore devoid of value and respect."

We are living now in a somewhat awesome age, in which new technologies like *in vitro* fertilization, gene-splicing, surrogate and artificial wombs, cloning, commercial patented life forms, embryo transplants, embryo fusion, and other experimental procedures carry the potential consequences of the abortion mentality beyond human comprehension.

Is anyone there? Does anyone see what I see? Does anyone care?

CHAPTER 10

"I HAVE CALLED YOU BY YOUR NAME— YOU ARE MY BELOVED"
(Isaiah 43:1)
The Religious Dimension

"For God and before God, every human being is always unique and unrepeatable, somebody thought of and chosen from eternity, someone called and identified by his or her own name."

—Pope John Paul II

The Good News of God's Love

When God created this world, he saw in his mind's eye an infinite number of other possible worlds which he might have created. You and I were in some of those other possible worlds. We were not in others. But God did not want a world without you or me, because of his special predilection and love for us. It was as if God were saying, "Oh, I could have made a world without you, but I didn't want a world without you. No world for me would have been complete . . . without you."

It is also true that God could have chosen a world in which you did exist, but in circumstances and with gifts different from the actual circumstances of your life and with gifts other than your own. But he did not want "a different you." It is *this you* that God loves: the you with your actual fingerprints, hair color, voice and vision, with your unique and unrepeatable immortal soul.

God does not love us as one big glob of humanity. He loves each of us individually. In his own eyes there is no one and there never will be anyone like each of us. Our lives, and all the other individual circumstances and personal determinations of those lives, are God's special gift. His providence has chosen and destined you and me, by a special act of love, to deliver a message, to sing a song, and to confer an act of love on this world which no one else can. Each of us is a unique and unrepeatable image and likeness of God, a unique and unrepeatable mystery of his love.

Now God does not get new ideas or lose old

ones. This kind of change would imply imperfection. If God got a new idea it would mean that he was lacking at least that idea before it came to him. And if God were to lose an old idea, he would be missing some part of the knowledge that could be his. Both are impossible with God for he is all perfect and all knowing. The bottom theological line in this is that you and I, and the baby born in Akron, Ohio, have been known and loved by God from all eternity and through all eternity. Each of us has always been a part of the mind and heart of God. The "I" of God has been saying to the "Thou" of you and me an eternal "I love you."

The Testimony of Sacred Scripture

This is what God means when he speaks through the prophet Jeremiah: "I have loved you with an eternal love. This is why in loving kindness I have created you." (31:3) It was to this same Jeremiah that God said: "Before I formed you in the womb of your mother, I knew you. Before you were born I consecrated you; I appointed you a prophet to the nations." (Jeremiah 1:4-5) Saint Paul reflects this same eternal knowledge and love of God when he writes to the Galatians: "But when he who had set me apart, even before I was born, and called me through his grace, was pleased to reveal his Son in me, so that I might preach him among the gentiles . . . " (Galatians 1:15)

It is this same eternal knowledge and love of God that is reflected in Psalm 139, verses 13-16:

It was you who created my inmost self, and put me together in my mother's womb. For all these mysteries I thank you: for the wonder of myself, for the wonder of your works. You know me through and through, from having watched my bones take shape when I was being formed in secret, knitted together in the limbo of the womb. Your eyes beheld my unformed substance, and in your book they were all written: the days that were ordained for me, even before those days were begun.

Saint Paul also assures the Ephesians that "he has chosen us before the foundation of the world . . . and predestined us to adoption as his children through Jesus Christ according to the kind intention of his will." (1:4-5)

If all of this be true, that we have been known and loved in the mind and heart of God from all eternity and into all eternity, then it must also be true for those who have already begun their lives in the wombs of their mothers. Abba (Father) God has created the souls of these preborn babies and infused each of those souls into the egg of the human mother fertilized by the sperm of the human father. For God, at last an eternal dream has come true, an eternal vocation and predestination has become a reality in time.

God no doubt looks upon his child, the child he has loved from all eternity, with a delighted smile of his infinite love.

> Can a woman forget her nursing child, and have no compassion on the child of her womb? Even if a mother were to forget the child of her womb, I will never forget you. Look, I have carved you on the palms of my hands.
>
> (Isaiah 49:15-16)
>
> . . . for he who touches you, touches the apple of my eye.
>
> (Zechariah 2:8)

154

God, Abortion, and Human History

If God is indifferent to whether or not we kill this baby or allow it to live, then God does not care about the living or dying of any of us. If God does not love this baby, then the Good News is a cruel hoax, religion is a charade, and the Word of God is nothing more than a human invention, designed to deceive us.

In their remarkable book *Whatever Happened to the Human Race?* Francis Schaeffer and Dr. C. Everett Koop offer this final thought:

People are special and human life is sacred, whether or not we admit it. Every life is precious and worthwhile in itself—not only to us human beings but also to God. Every person is worth fighting for, regardless of whether he is young or old, sick or well, child or adult, born or unborn, or brown, red, yellow, black, or white.

If, in this last part of the twentieth century, the Christian community does not take a prolonged and vocal stand for the dignity of the individual and each person's right to life—for the right of each individual to be treated as created in the image of God, rather than as a collection of molecules with no unique value—we feel that as Christians we have failed the greatest moral test to be put before us in this century.

Future generations will look back, and many will either scoff or believe in Christ on the basis of whether we Christians of today took a sacrifical stand in our various walks of life on these overwhelmingly important issues. If we do not take a stand here and now, we certainly cannot lay any claim to being the salt of the earth in our generation.

. . . Will future generations look back and remember that—even if the twentieth century *did* end with a great surge of inhumanity—at least there was one group who stood consistently, whatever the price, for the value of the individual, thus passing on some

hope to future generations? Or are we Christians going to be merely swept along with the trends—our own moral values becoming increasingly befuddled, our own moral apathy reflecting the apathy of the world around us, our own inactivity sharing the inertia of the masses around us . . .? [pp. 195-98]

In her memorable article "The Lesson of Dachau," originally published in *Ladies' Home Journal,* September, 1945, the late journalist Dorothy Thompson wrote, "When I surveyed Dachau, my soul trembled within me." Her soul trembled at the fact that some of the prisoners willingly cooperated with their captors in the killing. She remarks that the loss of humanity was experienced among the prisoners, trying to bargain for their lives, as well as by the Nazi architects of these camps. She notes that these Nazi architects were highly educated men. In their libraries could be found the finest classical literature. On their pianos, the finest classical music. On their walls hung examples of the finest classical art. She suggested that there might be one thing missing from their homes: There would be no crucifixes, no religious symbols, no suggestion of the presence of God. At the end of her article, she reflects, "I am beginning to think that when God goes, all goes."

Viktor Frankl, one of Europe's best-known psychiatrists and a prisoner of a Nazi concentration camp himself, makes a similar observation about faith. Writing in his book *Man's Search for Meaning* (Beacon Press, 1959), Dr. Frankl insists that when a prisoner had a deep and authentic faith in God, he was in touch with something that enabled him to maintain his very humanity.

WE CAN'T JUST STAND THERE . . . WE HAVE TO DO SOMETHING!

"It all seemed so wrong. I said to myself, 'Somebody ought to do something about this!' Then I realized that I am somebody."

—Anonymous

What Can I Do? A Human Life Amendment

If you are there (still with me) and you see what I see, I'm sure that you will care. And I trust that you will ask with me: "What can I do?" When the Lord of Life asks, "Whom can I send?" I trust you will join me in my response: "Here I am. Send me." None of us can make it alone. We must go into this together.

Those who have been involved in the pro-life struggle are agreed that the only final guarantee of legal protection for all human life will be a *Human Life Amendment to the U.S. Constitution.* It is the only certain way to reverse the terrible effects of the Supreme Court decision. But before we get into specific recommendations for action, it might help to review how abortion-on-request became the law of the land and how this can be reversed by a Human Life Amendment.

Article III of the Constitution of the United States gives the federal courts power to rule in cases involving constitutional rights. A Texas woman claimed that the Texas state laws limiting abortions violated her constitutional rights. A district court agreed with the woman's contentions, saying that Texas laws infringed on the woman's Ninth and Fourteenth Amendment rights to liberty, privacy, and due process of law. In defense of its own state laws, the state of Texas argued that the unborn child is a person and has a constitutional right to life. The state appealed to the United States Supreme Court.

The Supreme Court, in a seven-to-two ruling, decided against the state of Texas and declared that the fetus is not legally a person under the

Fourteenth Amendment interpretations and therefore is not to be granted a right to life. The Court further decided that the woman was correct in her claims and stated that the Texas laws did indeed deny her right to liberty, privacy, and due process of law. The Court then decided that the state could in fact make no laws prohibiting abortions. In effect, because of the decision of the Supreme Court, any woman wanting to kill her unborn child, and able to find a doctor to do the killing, could have an abortion at any time during her pregnancy.

A recent book, *The Brethren* (Simon & Schuster, 1980) by Bob Woodward and Scott Armstrong, discusses the relative abilities and interactions of the justices of the present Supreme Court. In the last pages of the book, Justice John Paul Stevens is pictured pondering his first year (1976) in the Court. He finds himself "accustomed to watching his colleagues make pragmatic rather than principled decisions—shading the facts, twisting the law, warping logic to reconcile the unreconcilable." Woodward and Armstrong add that, even if this was not what Stevens had anticipated, ". . . it was the reality." (Certainly it seems to have been the reality in the decision legalizing abortion-on-request.)

Joseph P. Witherspoon, professor of law at the University of Texas, assails the infidelity of the Supreme Court in interpreting the Constitution according to the mind of its framers. Witherspoon believes, as many others do, that the Court crudely imposed its own practical-solution meanings on the Constitution rather than deriving its interpretations from the Constitution and the intentions of its framers. In hearings before the House of Representatives subcommittee on civil and constitutional rights (Feb. 4, 1976), he testified:

> . . . the abortion decisions of 1973 are the most erroneous decisions in the history of constitutional adjudication by the Supreme Court. The essential fault or evil with *Wade* and *Bolton* is that they represent a clear repudiation by the Court of its fundamental obligation under the doctrine of the rule of law or justice under law which is to construe a constitutional provision in light of the actual purpose of its framers in proposing it. . . .
>
> The framers of these two amendments principally sought to protect every human being, including unborn children from the time of their conception. . . . This was not only a purpose of those framers; it was their principal purpose.
>
> . . . the Court in abandoning its duty under the rule of law or justice under law in human society provides constitutional protection and approval for the deliberate killing of millions of unborn human beings under a constitutional amendment that guarantees fundamental justice and equal protection under the law to all human beings. [Serial No. 46, Part 1, pp. 26-27]

Changing the Court's Ruling

A Supreme Court ruling on a constitutional matter can be overturned only by (1) a reinterpretation of the Constitution by the same or a subsequent Supreme Court, or (2) by an amendment to the Constitution, as the Fourteenth Amendment was adopted to reverse the Dred Scott decision. In this present matter the first of these methods of overturning a Supreme Court decision seems highly unlikely. However, the second appears a real possibility to stem the tides of death and to offer permanent legal protection for the lives of all human beings.

It should perhaps be mentioned here that an interim stop-gap measure has more recently been proposed. It is called the Human Life Statute. Please note that it does not provide a full and complete solution. It is only a provisory and temporary arrangement to diminish the number of killings by abortion until the permanent guarantee of a Human Life Amendment can be passed and ratified.

Briefly, the Human Life Statute, under consideration at this moment, would simply fill in the real or pretended ignorance of the Supreme Court. In delivering its outrageous decision of 1973, the Supreme Court (*Roe* v. *Wade*) said in effect, "We do not know when human life begins. Therefore we are striking down all state laws prohibiting abortions." If the Human Life Statute is passed by the Senate and the House of Representatives, it would equivalently say to the Court: "You came to your conclusion because you did not know when a human life begins. Well, we can tell you. There is strong scientific evidence and testimony that human life begins at conception."

The pro-life hope is that this would invalidate the Supreme Court ruling and enable individual states to redraft their own laws prohibiting or regulating abortion. Such a statute would no doubt be challenged by the strong pro-abortion forces, led by the American Civil Liberties Union, the Planned Parenthood Federation of America, the National Abortion Rights Action League, the National Organization of Women, the Rockefeller

Foundation, and so forth. It could well be that the present Supreme Court would declare that such a statute is itself unconstitutional.

However, it is certainly worth the effort, even if it saves only one life. The Human Life Statute, introduced in the Senate (Senate Bill #158) by Senator Jesse Helms of North Carolina and in the House of Representatives (HR Bill #900) by Congressman Henry J. Hyde of Illinois and Romano L. Mazzoli of Kentucky, reads as follows:

HUMAN LIFE STATUTE

Section I. The Congress finds that present day scientific evidence indicates a significant likelihood that actual life exists from conception.

The Congress further finds that the fourteenth amendment to the Constitution of the United States was intended to protect all human beings.

Upon the basis of these findings, and in the exercise of the powers of the Congress, including its power under section 5 of the fourteenth amendment to the Constitution of the United States, the Congress hereby declares that for the purpose of enforcing the obligation of the States under the fourteenth amendment not to deprive persons of life without due process of law, human life shall be deemed to exist from conception, without regard to race, sex, age, health, defect, or condition of dependency; and for this purpose "person" shall include all human life as defined herein.

Section 2. Notwithstanding any other provision of law, no inferior federal court ordained and established by Congress under article III of the Constitution of the United States shall have jurisdiction to issue any restraining order, temporary or permanent injunction, or declaratory judgment in any case involving or arising from any State law or municipal ordinance that (1) protects rights of human persons between conception and birth, or (2) prohibits, limits, or regulates (a) the performance of abortions or (b) the provision at public expense of funds, facilities, personnel, or other assistance for the performance of abortions.

Section 3. If any provision of this Act or the application thereof to any person or circumstance is judicially determined to be invalid, the validity of the remainder of the Act and the application of such provision to other persons and circumstances shall not be affected by such determination.

The rub is that such a statute would leave the matter of legislation up to the individual states who would redraft their own laws. There could possibly be "abortion capitals" such as New York was under the late pro-abortion governor, Nelson Rockefeller. Such abortion capitals resulted from the propaganda and pressures described by Dr. Nathanson who was originally involved in this effort to overturn the law. Consequently, a statute would clearly not provide a complete and final solution.

The Human Life Amendment

Obviously the words used in a Human Life Amendment are not words carved in stone. One such proposed amendment reads this way:

HUMAN LIFE AMENDMENT

Section 1. The right to life is the paramount and most fundamental right of a person.

Section 2. With respect to the right to life guaranteed to persons by the fifth and fourteenth articles of amendment to the Constitution, the word "person" applies to all human beings, irrespective of age, health, function or condition of dependency, including their unborn offspring at every stage of their biological development including fertilization.

Section 3. No unborn person shall be deprived of life by any person: Provided, however, that nothing in this article shall prohibit a law permitting only those medical procedures required to prevent the death of a pregnant woman; but this law must require every reasonable effort be made to preserve the life and health of the unborn child.

Section 4. Congress and the several States shall have power to enforce this article by appropriate legislation.

Article V of the Constitution gives both the Congress and state legislatures the power to propose amendments to the Constitution. A congressional proposal, which is valid only when a majority of each house is in attendance, requires the approval of two-thirds of the voting members of the Senate and the House of Representatives. Every single amendment which has thus far in our history become law was introduced and begun in this manner.

An alternate procedure, which also could lead to such a Human Life Amendment, requires that the legislators of two-thirds of the states apply to Congress to call a Constitutional Convention for the purpose of proposing an amendment. This approach has never been attempted and, in the judgment of some, would probably present several legal problems which themselves would have to be submitted to the courts. This whole question seems so vitally important to our country that many people versed in the law do not want it entrusted to appointed judges, but insist that it must be decided by all the people of this country.

After a Human Life Amendment has been proposed, it must be ratified either by the legislators of three-fourths of the states or by conventions in three-fourths of the states. Although the Constitution does not specify how soon after proposal an amendment must be ratified, Congress may choose to set such a limit.

The Proposal and Ratification of the Amendment

A Human Life Amendment, if proposed by Congress, may be initiated in either house of Congress. If the amendment is begun in the House of Representatives, it is given the designation "H. J. Res."—House joint resolution. If it is introduced in the Senate: "S. J. Res."—Senate joint resolution.

Since the Human Life Statute has already been introduced in Congress, and with the impetus of a pro-life administration in this country, the next session of Congress is going to be a crucial time for a Human Life Amendment.

Consequently, it is a very appropriate time for us to write to our senators and congressmen, to urge their support of a Human Life Amendment. We must urge them to reverse the United States Supreme Court decision on abortion and to begin the process of restoring legal protection to pre-born human beings. In such letters (or visits if possible) we must tell our senators and congressmen that we would be very pleased to see them either sponsor such legislation or to add their names to legislation for life already introduced.

We can't be satisfied until we see some concrete action on the part of those who represent us. If they should decline our requests, we must tell them of our regret and disappointment in them as our senators or congressmen. In such letters, it is advisable to be controlled, logical, and yet forceful, without the expression of angry and explosive emotions that politicians easily dismiss as the work and words of a fanatic. Such letters should be brief, and, if they are ended with a question, there will be added assurance of an answer.

After the Human Life Amendment is proposed by the Senate and by the House, it will then have to be ratified by three-fourths of the fifty states in the Union. This will require a majority consensus of the American people, an agreement that all human life should be protected by the law. And this means that our American people must be educated about the pertinent issues. The media at present tend to shadow and obscure the facts, and to promote indirectly public acceptance of abortion-on-request.

At least the following facts must be circulated, with a full explanation of the dehumanization process which is leading us to an acceptance of the New Ethic.

- Abortion is killing. In every abortion an innocent human being is killed. For a full understanding of this fact, the facts of fertilization and fetal development should be made known.

- The decision of the Supreme Court has legalized abortion during all nine months of pregnancy. The unborn have no status as human beings or persons before the law. Any woman who wants an abortion at any time during her pregnancy needs only to find a doctor who is willing to do the killing. If the woman is married, she has no obligation, according to the Court, to inform her husband or to seek his consent. If the woman is a minor, she has no need to have the permission of her parents to procure an abortion.

- There are currently 1.5 million abortions being performed each year in this country, which amounts to more than four thousand each day. The justification of these killings is strictly utilitarian. The deaths of these babies are solving problems. The babies are human sacrifices on the altars of convenience and economy. The end justifies the means.

- Having rationalized and legalized abortion, the proponents of the New Ethic, the quality-of-life ethic, are pushing now for the killing of the deformed, the retarded, the handicapped, and the aged.

It is very important for us to be informed so that we can assist in getting the word out and getting the truth before the people of our country. We must inform America about the evil of abortion. It is the only hope for a Human Life Amendment. And a Human Life Amendment is the only hope for our humanity and our civilization.

Included at the end of this book is a Basic Reading List. However, a good and easy-to-read overview of the situation is presented in *Handbook on Abortion* by Dr. and Mrs. J. C. Willke. If you can't find it at your local Christian bookstore, it can be ordered from the Hayes Publishing Company, 6304 Hamilton Avenue, Cincinnati, Ohio 45224. The cost of the paperback edition is currently $1.75 per book; quantity rates are available. I would also suggest that to remain current on the pertinent pro-life questions, one should subscribe to the *National Right to Life News,* Suite 341, National Press Building, 529 14th Street N.W., Washington, D.C. 20045. A one-year subscription at this time costs $12.00.

Final Suggestions for Pro-Life Activities

1. *Join a pro-life group.* In unity there is strength, but as individuals most of us can do very little. I think you should select the pro-life group you join according to a self-estimation of your own gifts. There is a place in the pro-life movement for everyone. You might consider speaking up in public. Perhaps you would prefer to join Birthright or Heartbeat as a counselor. Make a self-estimation of your own gifts and put them in the service of life. Someday you will be proud of your good judgment, courage, and basic decency. When people ask you, "Did you know? Did you do anything?" you can proudly say, "Indeed I did!"

2. *Financially support the pro-life effort.* The opposition is well organized and well funded. Most of the pro-life groups are struggling for survival. Many of us can organize a bake sale or a "run (or walk) for life." There are many ways to raise funds for life. Give your imagination a chance.

3. *Write.* Write brief and clear letters to news-

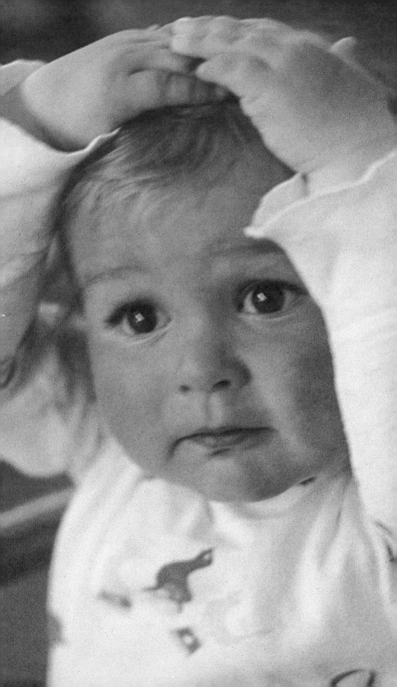

papers, television stations, magazines. Thank them for their honest and clear presentations of the pro-life struggle. Send them your regrets when you feel the news has been slanted or the language euphemistic. For example, "pro-choice" sounds great, doesn't it? What it means in effect is that the choice is to let your baby live or to kill it. That's not so great, is it? Ask the editors and the columnists not to hide behind the euphemisms but to bring the facts out into the open.

4. *Publicize and offer whatever assistance you can to groups providing alternatives to abortion.* We must extend our loving compassion to those with problem pregnancies if we are to be credible in our pro-life stance. A 28-minute cassette taken from a Christopher Closeup TV program and entitled "Alternative to Abortion" is currently available for $3.50 from The Christophers, 12 East 48th Street, New York, New York 10017. Usually, wherever abortion clinics run their advertisements, those who are promoting alternatives to abortion also have ads. Birthright and Heartbeat are two such organizations. Contact them and ask how you can help, according to your own gifts, inclinations, and available time.

5. *Be sure to take part in any pro-life marches or conventions which you can attend.* We all need our batteries charged. And sometimes, due to the bias of the media, we can tend to feel defeated or even be led to feel that we are fighting a losing cause. A public display of our unity in the cause of life is a contagious experience. It will help us personally, and it will be an eloquent statement to the country at large.

6. *Ask your church pastor or minister or the rabbi of your synagogue to preach on the right to life.* Ask him/her if there is a pro-life group organized in the parish or congregation. If not, why not? Many pastors, ministers, and rabbis are a bit diffident and would be greatly helped to feel the support and encouragement of your opinion.

7. *Get the message into the schools.* Most pro-life groups have a "speakers bureau" available to go to organizations and schools. It is vitally important to get the pro-life message to the young, who are constantly pressured to become sexually active in spite of all the destructive results of this pressure. If you and your group can instruct competent high school boys and girls to present the pro-life argumentation to their peers, it would be especially effective. In various places in our country, the "Youth for Life" groups are proving capable and confident in bringing the pro-life message to their own age groups.

8. *Keep the life-death issues visible.* Wear a pro-life rose appliqué on your lapel. (One source of these appliqué's is IDEA, P.O. Box 119, Elmwood Park, Illinois 60635.) Wear a pro-life bracelet on your wrist. Put a pro-life sticker on the bumper of your car. Put pro-life stickers on the envelopes you mail out. There is a deluge of pro-abortion propaganda drenching our contemporary society. It is extremely important that we keep visible the cause of life, belief in the sanctity and sacredness of every human life.

9. *Celebrate life.* I wish the churches and synagogues would have special celebrations of conception. Perhaps groups could even plan their own

rituals and organize parties to celebrate the gift of new life. We should also celebrate birthdays and anniversaries and give a very special homage and sign of appreciation to the aged. We are pygmies standing on the shoulders of giants. We owe the aged our loving gratitude and congratulations.

10. *Perhaps most important of all, we must pray.* We should be praying for everyone involved in this drama of life and death, this national clarification of values. We should be praying for the women with problem pregnancies, for the courage and conviction of medical doctors, for those unfortunate men and women who have been deluded into accepting the abortion solution of their problems. We should pray for one another that we do not lose courage, that our motivation be always positive, and that our efforts be always acts of love. Saint Augustine once said that "prayer is the strength of man and the weakness of God." Finally, it was Saint Ignatius of Loyola who counseled us: "Work as if everything depends on you. Pray as if everything depends on God."

EPILOGUE

At the beginning of this book, I asked you as a personal favor to me to stay with me, to hear my fears and to share my sorrow. Now I would like to thank you for your act of love. It has been said that we may forget those we have laughed with, but we can never forget those with whom we have cried. Having you as a companion on this journey through some past days of my life and into the labyrinths of my emotions is a consolation that will always be for me a grateful memory. I hope that you, too, have been enriched in the sharing of these thoughts and emotions. I feel that somehow we have joined hands and climbed a high hill together.

At the beginning of the book, I also said that you may not be where I am, and that we might still be somewhat distant from each other even at the end. If so, I am ready to listen and to read and to walk with you to where you are.

John Noonan, a lawyer, and Mildred Jefferson, a physician, two special heroes of the pro-life struggle, are agreed that a cause like this one "occurs only once in a century." It is truly a crossroads moment in our history, a turning point, a day of decision. Historians will someday look back on these days and ask the inevitable questions: Did you know? Did you speak up for life? Or did you turn your head, pretending to be an innocent bystander?

And those of us who believe in a Day of Divine Judgment know that these questions will be asked also by the Lord of Life who takes as done to himself whatever we do for the least of his children.

Were you there? Did you see? Did you care?

For myself, I have left all the timetables and the final results in God's hands. But however and whenever we come to the moment of our enlightenment and to the end of the struggle, when human historians and the angel of God record those who spoke up for the babies, the handicapped, the retarded, the aged, and the forgotten, I hope that my name will be written on that scroll in bold letters. I want my life to be a voice for the voiceless, a defense for the defenseless, and a caring love for the unloved and the unwanted.

So I have vowed to wear my pro-life bracelet as a symbol of this life commitment. I have never and will never take it off. I want to wear that symbol of reverence for life in all the days of my life and in death.

On the lapel of my suit I also wear a red rose appliqué, with the word *life* embroidered under the rose. The rose is a pro-life symbol. I wear it as a sign of my unconditional commitment to the struggle and of my unconditional love for every member of our human family, born and unborn.

And I do believe that, no matter how long it takes to clarify our values, as a human family we will find our way into the light. We will someday see each life as a unique and unrepeatable image and likeness of God, a fragile miracle of his love, bringing us a special message from God himself. We will realize that our lives are shaped by those who love us . . . and by those who refuse to love us.

I think that this is what the poet John Donne meant when he wrote, "No man is an island . . . "

and what Jesus meant when he said, "All I ask of you is that you love one another." If we are faithful, someday . . . someday the rose of life will bloom in all of its magnificent beauty, for all of us to behold and to love.

Somehow Bette Midler's song, from the motion picture of the same name, seems to say it all:

THE ROSE

Some say love—it is a river that drowns the
   tender reed,
Some say love—it is a razor that leaves your soul
   to bleed,
Some say love—it is a hunger, an endless
   aching need,
I say love—it is a flower, and you its only seed.

It's the heart afraid of breaking that never learns
   to dance,
It's the dream afraid of waking that never takes
   the chance,
It's the one who won't be taken, who cannot
   seem to give,
And the soul afraid of dying that never learns
   to live.

When the night has been too lonely, and the road
   has been too long,
And you think that love is only for the lucky and
   the strong,
Just remember in the winter, far beneath the
   bitter snows,
Lies the seed that with the sun's love in the spring
   becomes the rose.

Please remember me as loving you.

John Powell, S.J.

BASIC READING LIST

Brown, Harold O. J. *Death Before Birth*. Nashville: Thomas Nelson, 1977.

Connery, John, S.J. *Abortion: The Development of the Roman Catholic Perspective*. Chicago: Loyola University Press, 1977.

Cox, Archibald. *The Role of the Supreme Court in American Government*. New York: Oxford University Press, 1976.

Denes, Magda. *In Necessity and Sorrow: Life and Death in an Abortion Hospital*. New York: Basic Books, 1976.

Diamond, Eugene, M.D. *This Curette for Hire*. Chicago: ACTA Foundation, 1977.

Flanagan, Geraldine. *The First Nine Months of Life*. New York: Simon & Schuster, 1962.

Garton, Jean S. *Who Broke the Baby?* Minneapolis: Bethany Fellowship, 1979.

Granfield, David. *The Abortion Decision*. New York: Doubleday, 1969.

Grisez, Germain. *Abortion: The Myths, the Realities, and the Arguments*. New York: Corpus Books, 1970.

Hilgers, Thomas, and Horan, Dennis J. (eds.). *Abortion and Social Justice*. Mission, Kansas: Andrews & McMeel, 1973.

Hilgers, Thomas; Horan, Dennis; and Mall, David (eds.). *New Perspectives on Human Abortion*. Washington, D.C.: University Publications of America, 1981.

Mall, David, and Watts, Walter, M.D. *The Psychological Aspects of Abortion*. Washington, D.C.: University Publications of America, 1979.

Menninger, Karl, M.D. *Whatever Became of Sin?* New York: Hawthorn Books, 1973.

Nathanson, Bernard N., M.D., and Ostling, Richard N. *Aborting America*. New York: Doubleday, 1979.

Noonan, John T., Jr. *A Private Choice: Abortion in America in the Seventies*. New York: Free Press, 1979.

Ramsey, Paul. *Ethics at the Edges of Life*. New Haven: Yale University Press, 1978.

Rice, Charles E. *The Vanishing Right to Live*. New York: Doubleday, 1969.

Schaeffer, Francis A., and Koop, C. Everett, M.D. *What-*

ever Happened to the Human Race? Old Tappan, N.J.: Fleming H. Revell, 1979.

Summerhill, Louise. *The Story of Birthright: The Alternative to Abortion.* Kenosha: Prow Books, 1973.

Wakin, Edward. *Helping the Unwed Mother.* Chicago: Claretian Publications, 1976.

Walling, Regis. *When Pregnancy Is a Problem.* St. Meinrad, Indiana: Abbey Press, 1980.

Willke, Dr. and Mrs. John C. *Handbook on Abortion,* rev. ed. Cincinnati: Hayes Publishing Co., 1975.

ACKNOWLEDGMENTS *Continued from page ii*

Statement by Dr. R. A. Gallop is reprinted by permission of Dr. Gallop, 191 Dromore Avenue, Winnipeg, R3M OH9, Manitoba, Canada.

Excerpts from "Death, Euthanasia and Parental Consent" by Richard E. Harbin, in *Pediatric Nursing*, Vol. 2, No. 4 (July/August 1976), pp. 26–28. Material excerpted with permission of Richard E. Harbin and the publisher of *Pediatric Nursing*.

Excerpt from "Editor's Corner" by Dan Lyons, in *Christian Crusade Weekly* (1979). Reprinted by permission of Billy James Hargis, Editor, *Christian Crusade Weekly*, Tulsa, Oklahoma.

Lyrics for "The Rose" by Amanda McBroom. © 1977 and 1979 by Fox Fanfare Music, Inc. All rights reserved. Used by permission.

Excerpt from a personal communication (1961) from Margaret Mead, quoted in *Psychiatry and Ethics* by Maurice Levine (George Braziller, 1972). Reprinted by permission of George Braziller.

Excerpts from the pamphlet *Pro-Life Work and Social Justice* by Francis X. Meehan (National Conference of Catholic Bishops' Committee for Pro-Life Activities, 1980). Reprinted by permission of the National Conference of Catholic Bishops, Washington, D.C.

Excerpts from the keynote address by Dr. Bernard Nathanson at the 1980 National Right to Life Convention in Anaheim, California, copyright © 1980 by Bernard Nathanson. Reprinted by permission of Dr. Bernard Nathanson.

Excerpts from *Aborting America* by Bernard N. Nathanson and Richard N. Ostling. Copyright © 1979 by Bernard N. Nathanson and Richard N. Ostling. Reprinted by permission of Doubleday & Co., Inc.

Statistics for chart ("A Grim Memorial Day Reminder of American War Casualties") compiled by Barbara Syska, Research Analyst, National Right to Life Committee. Reprinted by permission of the National Right to Life Committee, Washington, D.C.

Excerpt from *Beyond Abortion: The Theory and Practice of the Secular State* by Charles E. Rice (Franciscan Herald Press, 1979). Reprinted by permission of Franciscan Herald Press, Chicago, Ill. 60609.

Excerpts from *Whatever Happened to the Human Race?* by Francis A. Schaeffer and C. Everett Koop, M.D. Copyright © 1979 by Franky Schaeffer V Productions, Inc. Published by Fleming H. Revell Company. Used by permission.

Excerpt from an unpublished speech by Rev. George Tribou, given at a March of Dimes dinner in Little Rock, Arkansas, January 31, 1980. Reprinted by permission of Rev. George Tribou.